Exploring the
Tualatin River Basin

A Nature and Recreation Guide

by the Tualatin Riverkeepers

Edited by Susan Peter, Shirley Ewart, Barbara Schaffner

Shirley Ewart

Barbara Schaffner

D1026174

Paddling the Tualatin. Photo by Michael Wilhelm

Oregon State University Press
Corvallis Oregon

Susan Peter

The paper in this book meets the guidelines for permanence and durability of the Committee on Production Guidelines for Book Longevity of the Council on Library Resources and the minimum requirements of the American National Standard for Permanence of Paper for Printed Library Materials Z39.48-1984.

Library of Congress Cataloging-in-Publication Data
Exploring the Tualatin River Basin : a nature and recreation guide /
Tualatin Riverkeepers ; Susan Peter and Shirley Ewart, editors—1st ed.
    p. cm.
Includes bibliographical references (p.)
    ISBN 0-87071-540-2
1. Natural history—Oregon—Tualatin River Watershed—Guidebooks.
2. Tualatin River Watershed (Or.)—Guidebooks. I. Peter, Susan, 1947-
II. Ewart, Shirley. III. Tualatin Riverkeepers.

QH105.O7 E86 2002
796.5'09795—dc21

2001055414

Oregon State University Press
101 Waldo Hall
Corvallis OR 97331-6407
541-737-3166 fax 541-737-3170
www.oregonstate.edu/dept/press

OREGON STATE
UNIVERSITY

Front cover photo: Green Heron by Michael Wilhelm.
Back cover: Paddling the Tualatin by Michael Wilhelm, River Otter by Jim Cruce.

CONTENTS

CONTENTS, continued

ACKNOWLEDGEMENTS

Tualatin Riverkeepers would like to thank the many people who made this book possible. Birdwatchers, botanists, explorers, paddlers, and writers, we couldn't have produced this without you!

Created by the Tualatin Riverkeepers

Editors
Shirley Ewart, Susan Peter, and Barbara Schaffner

Contributors
Dana Abel
Bruce Barbarasch
Joe Blowers
Jack Broome
Nathalie Darcy
Shari Exo
Greg Gillson
Lori Hennings
Laura Hill
Jim Rapp
Jere Retzer
Doug Robberson
Julie Rose
Kendra Smith
Mel Waggy
Tom Wolf

Features
Greg Baker
John A. Christy
Steve Engel
Shirley Ewart
Thomas Love
Bob Paulson
Brian Wegener
Paul Whitney
Kim Wilson

Illustrations
Steve Engel
Deepa Kadkade
Karlene Lusby
Barbara Macomber

Photographers
Steve Berliner
Jim Cruce
Susan Peter
Monte Rumgay
Brian Wegener
Michael Wilhelm

Maps & Plant Scans
Susan Peter

Graphic Design
BeBop Graphics

Proofreaders
Carolyn Goldwasser
Charlie Quinn
Marilyn Stinnett

THE TUALATIN RIVERKEEPERS

The Tualatin Riverkeepers is a community-based organization working to protect and restore Oregon's Tualatin River system. The Tualatin Riverkeepers promotes watershed stewardship through public education, public access, community involvement, and advocacy.

The Tualatin Riverkeepers' goals are accomplished through organizing public tours of the river including the Annual Tualatin River Discovery Day; by providing educational programs to community groups and schools; and by providing community involvement opportunities in clean-up, issue advocacy, and river and watershed observational monitoring.

This guide is a result of the work of many individuals and groups who also strive to help The Tualatin Riverkeepers realize these goals. We hope it will encourage you to take an active part in protecting and enjoying this wonderful river system.

Sue Marshall
Executive Director, the Tualatin Riverkeepers
www.tualatinriverkeepers.org
info@tualatinriverkeepers.org
16507 SW Roy Rogers Road
Sherwood, OR 97140

Editor Shirley Ewart enjoys a paddle on the Tualatin River.
Photo by Michael Wilhelm

SPONSORS

The Tualatin Riverkeepers thanks the following sponsors
whose contributions made this book possible:

NW Natural

EPSON

Meyer Memorial Trust

Tualatin Hills Park and Recreation District

Tualatin Valley Water Quality
Endowment Fund of the Oregon Community Foundation

FOREWORD

*"Open-space planning should take its cue from the patterns of nature itself...
the flood plains...and above all, the streams. Fortuitously, they are probably the
best looking parts of our local landscape. Stream valleys are the best connectors of
all. Where the water flows, the positive benefits of open space are the clearest...If we
follow this track in our open-space planning, we are at once securing the prime
lands and the lands which give linkage and continuity—in a word, regional design."*

—— William H. Whyte, *The Last Landscape*, 1968

Few people have had a more significant influence on regional planning in
America than the late William H. Whyte. Whyte was known for his seminal
research on public use of urban spaces and his book *The Last Landscape* was
a singular inspiration for our own Portland region open spaces initiative.

Without question, The Tualatin Riverkeepers, more than any other group,
embraces Whyte's admonition to follow the water "Where the positive
benefits of open space are the clearest." With their *Exploring the Tualatin River
Basin: A Nature and Recreation Guide,* the Riverkeepers have a wonderful tool
to enlist a new legion of stream and river keepers throughout the Tualatin
Basin. As Portland Parks Director Charles Jordan says, "Those who do not
know will not care. Those who do not care, will not act." I feel strongly that
it will only be those who develop an intimate knowledge of the special
places like those that are described in this book, who will be the next
generation of greenspace advocates and stewards. For that we owe a great
debt to the Tualatin Riverkeepers.

The most frequently asked questions we get at Audubon Society of Portland,
are "where can I go to find...? I have a friend in visiting from New York
and I want to take them bird watching; where can I see birds in Beaverton?"
While there are other natural history guides to the metropolitan region, like
our own *Wild in the City: a guide to Portland's natural areas*, the Tualatin
Riverkeepers' guide is the most comprehensive and authoritative reference
to the Tualatin Basin.

The Tualatin Riverkeepers have uncovered sites I have never heard of, much
less gone to. And, I've been wandering around the basin for the better part
of twenty years. The watershed locator maps, color photographs, and
detailed wildlife and amenity information all contribute to a wonderful field
guide to natural areas of the Tualatin Basin.

—— Mike Houck
Urban Naturalist, Audubon Society of Portland
Co-editor, *Wild in the City: a guide to Portland's natural areas*

Viewing Tips

Plants do a pretty good job of holding still, but viewing animals can be more challenging.

These tips might help:

Be patient and quiet. If a viewing blind is not available, consider alternate methods of camouflaging your presence, such as standing quietly between two trees.

Birds show their brightest and most flamboyant plumage during mating season. Prepare, so you know what to expect and when.

Plan evening outings to see and hear nocturnal creatures, like bats, owls, and beavers.

Birds, deer, and other wildlife are most active in the early morning and evening twilight hours.

Use your sense of smell and touch to fully appreciate plants.

Before your outing, take some time with a field guide. Learn how to use it, and what you might want to look for.

Many parks have useful notice boards with maps and tips for identifying the local species.

Our index is coded for illustrations and descriptions, with page numbers in bold or italics, respectively, to aid in identification.

Leave your dog home. Pets can hinder wildlife viewing.

Be a good sport:

Stay on posted trails. Do not cause erosion by shortcutting on switchbacks.

Do not pick flowers or remove anything other than trash from public parks.

Do not touch injured or baby animals.

Never approach or feed wildlife, even if they appear to be begging. "People food" inhibits animals and birds from foraging for those foods best suited for their health.

Checklist of what to take along:

Water and snacks

Insect repellent

Rain jacket

Comfortable shoes

Long pants and long sleeves to protect against sunburn, insect bites, and vegetation

Binoculars and magnifying glass

Field identification guides and a good street map

Trash bag to carry out litter, your own and what you find along the trail.

Every effort has been made to assure current and accurate information. Please notify us where it needs updating. Please also let us know if we have given you information that has helped provide an especially memorable experience. 503-590-5813 or info@tualatinriverkeepers.org

Sincerely,

Shirley Ewart, Susan Peter, and Barbara Schaffner, Editors

How to Use This Guide

Please take a moment to look at the overview map on pages x and xi. Color is used to differentiate the 10 geographic areas covered by the book.

Special Features: Writings on the wildlife, ecology, and history of the Tualatin River Basin can be found throughout the guide. Look for the color-washed pages to find them at a glance. There is also a comprehensive paddle guide.

Chapters: There are 10 chapters corresponding to 10 geographic areas of the Tualatin River Basin. These areas are arranged around watersheds, starting upstream in the Coast Range and continuing in an orderly arrangement to the Willamette River. Each area is prefaced by a local map and a brief overview. The numbers correspond to the featured sites. Most sites are city parks, some are private property open to public use, and a few have restricted use. Some sites are meant to be viewed only from the perimeter.

Site Descriptions: Please read them to ensure that your needs and expectations will be met. These sites offer opportunity for a wide range of uses: you may want to take a couple of toddlers to a neighborhood park, lead a group of kids into a wild swamp to study nature, or find a quiet place to relax and observe birds. Each site is unique in its size, level of development, and the expanse and type of its natural area. Not all sites have trails, but those that do, generally have trails that are 1/4 to 1/2 mile in length unless otherwise noted.

Directions: Each site description includes access information, but take along an up-to-date road map; it may also be necessary.

Icons: Preceding each site description are icons indicating the type of wildlife that can be found there. Amenity icons are at the end of each article.

Bibliography and Index: At the back of this guide you will find an index keyed for photographs and descriptions, plus Latin name cross-referencing for plant species.

WILDLIFE ICONS

 Songbirds   Waterfowl   Wading Birds   Birds of Prey

 Small Mammals   Freshwater Mammals   Hoofed Mammals   Carnivorous Mammals   Reptiles/ Amphibians   Fish   Wildflowers

AMENITY ICONS

 Parking   Restrooms   Handicapped Access   Hiking   Picnic

 Camping   Boat Ramp   Small Boats   Playground   No Dogs

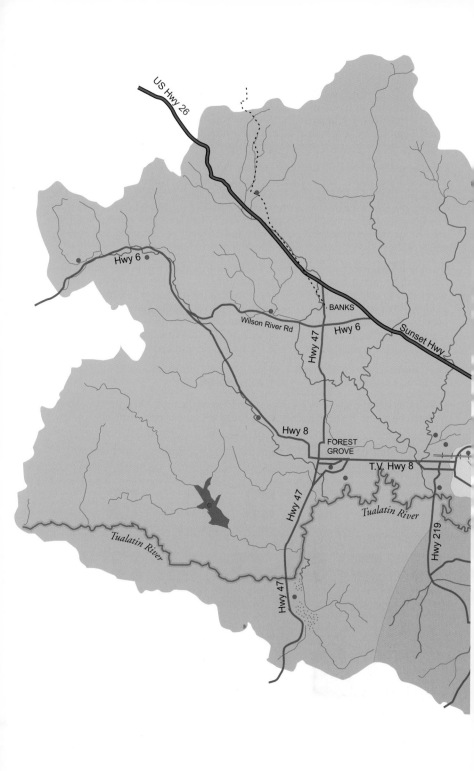

VIEWING AREA 1: Upper Tualatin River

Most of the water in this stretch of the Tualatin River comes from the Coast Range. Barney Reservoir, high in these mountains, gathers water for the Trask River, but not all of it is destined to flow west to the ocean through Tillamook County. Some is artificially diverted to the east side of the ridge, adding to the headwaters of the Tualatin high above Cherry Grove.

The main stem joins creeks with such picturesque names as Sunday, Maple, and Roaring, coming down from Grindstone Ridge, Skunk Hollow, and Timbuktu. Scoggins, Carpenter, and Gales creeks, with tributary creeks named Lousignout, Finger, Parsons, Coffee, and Deep, also flow into the Tualatin River before it reaches Forest Grove.

Dairy Creek, the Tualatin's single greatest contributing system, comes from north of Forest Grove. Its West Fork passes through Manning and Buxton at Sunset Highway where it joins streams from such places as Poliwaski and Paisley canyons. The East Fork of Dairy Creek begins near Snooseville Corner and Plentywater Creek. The two forks join together in the farmland just north of Verboort.

McKay Creek, starting above North Plains, gathers together various Hillsboro creeks before joining the huge Dairy Creek system. Dairy Creek passes under Highway 8 just west of Hillsboro. South of Hillsboro it joins the Tualatin River just to the west of Jackson Bottom Slough.

U. J. Hamby Park (see page 16).
Photo by Susan Peter

VIEWING AREA 1: Upper Tualatin River

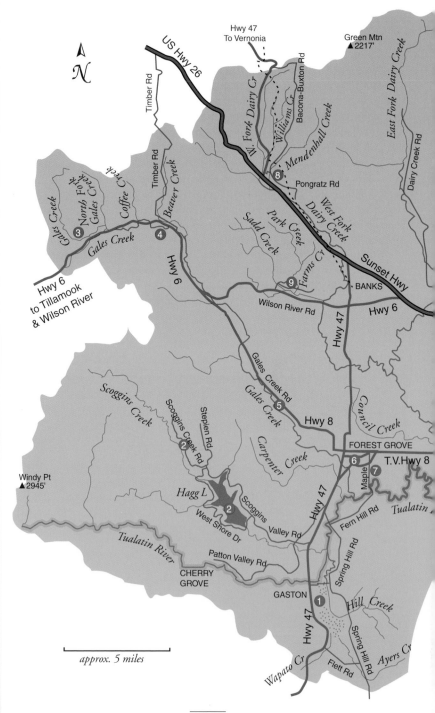

VIEWING AREA 1: Upper Tualatin River

Viewing Sites

1. Wapato Lake
2. Hagg Lake
3. Gales Creek Campground
4. Blodgett Arboretum
5. Rippling Waters Nature Park
6. Rodgers Park
7. Fernhill Wetlands
8. Banks-Vernonia State Trail
9. Cedar Canyon Marsh/Killin Wetlands
10. U. J. Hamby Park
11. Glencoe Swale
12. Jackson Bottom Wetland Preserve

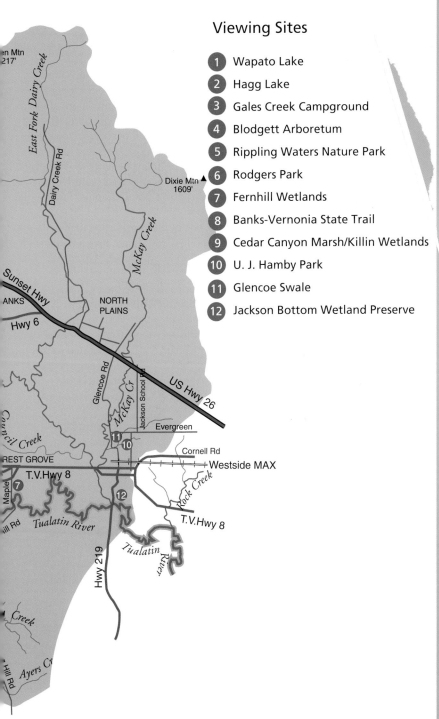

1 WAPATO LAKE FLOODED FARMLANDS

A Winter Wonderland Tour from Forest Grove to Gaston and Cornelius

This 20-mile loop tour is best taken in winter, when the Tualatin River overflows its banks to flood adjacent farm fields. Most of this land is privately owned and not open for public access. However, at several places along this route there are good wide shoulders that allow you to pull over and view the waterfowl.

During the winter months this area hosts thousands of waterfowl. Pintails and coots are plentiful, but the highlight of this tour is a very large flock of up to 3,000 Tundra Swans. Expert birders may also find a few Trumpeter Swans among the flock.

Start at Fernhill Wetlands (see page 12), one of the best birding spots in the Tualatin Basin. From there, travel south on Fern Hill Road; turn left on Spring Hill Road, and continue south past Gaston Road. Wapato Lake is on the right side of the road.

Wapato Lake was a favorite of the Atfalati people. Here they gathered wapato, a tuberous plant that was a staple in their diet. In 1852, Chief Ki-A-Kuts of the Atfalati negotiated with the U. S. federal government to have Wapato Lake and the surrounding area as their reservation. Congress never ratified this treaty, and the last of the Atfalati were eventually relocated to the Grand Ronde reservation under a new treaty. (See *The Atfalati* on page 21.) Since then, Wapato Lake has been drained to grow other crops, but in the winter the old lakebed floods, attracting thousands of waterfowl and dozens of hunters.

After scanning the lake with binoculars, continue south on Spring Hill Road. Turn right onto Flett Road and continue to Highway 47. Along Flett Road look for wading Great Blue Herons or Great Egrets.

Turn north on Highway 47 and drive up the west side of Wapato Lake. When you get to Gaston, stop and park at the baseball field on Gaston Road, just east of Highway 47 on your right. (There are portable toilets here.) Walk east along Gaston Road for about 0.7 miles. You may see flocks of Canada Geese and Northern Pintails overhead. On the water, south of the road, you are likely to see Buffleheads and Lesser Scaup. Back at the baseball field, just beyond the outfield, you may find Common Snipe. Walk along Highway 47 through Gaston for better views of ducks, geese, and swans on Wapato Lake and in the surrounding marshy areas.

When you return to your car continue north on Highway 47. The flooded farm fields east of the road are another good place to look for swans. If you should spot some, the shoulder is wide enough for parking. Still looking for Tundra Swans? From Highway 8 in the town of Cornelius, turn south onto 10th Avenue, which becomes Golf Course Road. Continue south and look for swans on the flooded fields to the east of the road. This will add 4.5 miles to the tour.

*Right photo
by Dana Abel*

*Below photo
by Sue Marshall*

Ki-A-Kuts Falls (above) received its current name during a June 21, 1999 dedication ceremony. Officials from the Confederate Tribes of the Grand Ronde gave their blessing and urged all to "take a moment to look around – the water, the earth, all things – reflect on the circle – the circle of life."

From left to right: Don Day, Leon "Chips" Tom, and Tony Johnson.

2 HAGG LAKE

Hagg Lake is popular year-round. During the fishing season anglers cast for rainbow trout, steelhead, and bass. Summer is a great time to enjoy the trees and wildflowers, and bird watching is great all year. A wide, smooth road (with bike lanes) follows the shoreline all the way around this large lake. Remember to drive slowly; it is not uncommon to see deer crossing the highway.

To make a clockwise loop of 10.5 miles around the lake, turn left on West Shore Drive and cross over the dam. The first stop is immediately across the dam at the parking lot on the right. In the deep water are Double-crested Cormorants, Western Grebes, Ring-necked Ducks, and Lesser Scaups. Unusual winter birds include loons, Red-necked and Horned grebes, and Greater Scaups. Bald Eagles and Ospreys nest around the lake, and Northern Rough-winged Swallows and Purple Martins make their homes near the dam. In the grassy areas by the picnic tables, there are red and white clovers, tiny yellow hop clover, and pale mauve vetch; all are members of the Pea Family. Under the Douglas-firs look for sword fern, thimbleberry, and salal.

As you continue along West Shore Drive notice the Scotch broom. During the winter it is an inconspicuous dark green bush, but in June this widespread and invasive non-native blazes in golden glory. In the spring, migrant warblers, vireos, and swifts are plentiful around the woods between Lee Road and Sain Creek. Along the lakeshore, Wood Ducks nest in crevices in the maple trees. Listen for their squeaky calls. Watch for Common and Hooded mergansers in the quiet backwaters.

From the Sain Creek picnic grounds, you can catch the 15.5-mile round-the-lake trail. See the red trail markers? Follow them south and soon you will see thimbleberry, various saxifrages, salal, bearberry (kinnikinnick), and hazel which occupy shady areas. Around a bend enormous, lichen-covered Oregon white oaks stand sentry. Patches of purple iris are found there in the spring. Watch out for poison oak.

Farther around the lake, at Scoggins Creek picnic area, you may want to stop and look for American Dippers in the stream. Then, about a half-mile farther, on your left, watch for a rather complex road sign. Turn onto Stepien Road, and almost immediately onto Scoggins Valley Road East. On the right, 2.3 miles up the hill, is a wide pull-out. Park here and take a look around.

In August, you will find bright blue chicory and yellow St. John's wort, a non-native widely used in herbal medicine as a calmative. Berries on the evergreen and Himalayan blackberries are ripe and the bracken fern is already golden-brown. You may also see the large, bright pink flowers of the sweet pea. Like the invasive Himalayan blackberry, this fairly common roadside plant has escaped from cultivation.

An Oregon myrtle stands prominently in this semi-clearing; its glossy evergreen leaves, when bruised, smell like bay leaves. This is a good habitat for common backyard birds, but you may also find Pileated Woodpeckers. In the summer there are vireos, flycatchers, thrushes, and grosbeaks. Overhead, look for Red-tailed Hawks, American Kestrels, and Cooper's Hawks.

Returning to the loop road around the lake, travel another mile to the mouth of Tanner Creek. This area is marshy and in summer has Red-winged Blackbirds and Yellow-breasted Chats, and occasionally Soras, Yellow Warblers, and Green Herons. In winter there are numerous waterfowl. Watch for unusual ducks like Eurasian Wigeons. There are several pull-outs here at the shallow north end of the lake.

The east side of the lake is more open, with grassy fields and oak knolls. Be sure to keep your eyes open for Western Bluebirds. Common birds in the blackberry tangles and old orchards are California Quail, sparrows, and Dark-eyed Juncos, but in the summer you may also see Lazuli Buntings and Chipping Sparrows. At night listen for the calls of Western Screech-, Northern Saw-whet, and Great Horned owls. Greg Gillson, our guide to Hagg Lake, has remarked on the enormous number and variety of birds in this area. We encourage explorers to take along binoculars and a good field guide.

Directions: From Forest Grove, 5 miles south on Highway 47. Turn on Scoggins Valley Road and travel 3.2 miles west to the park entrance. A day use fee is charged from late April through October.

Amenities:

Lazuli Bunting
with chicks.
*Photo by
Michael Wilhelm*

Purple iris.
Photo by Susan Peter

3 | GALES CREEK CAMPGROUND

Would you like to spend a quiet weekend, away from traffic, from the telephone and television, and yet still within Washington County? Then head for Gales Creek Campground. From here a six-mile trail leads north along Gales Creek and another extends westward toward Elk and King Mountains. These trails are closed to off-road vehicles. Just south of this campground is a spawning ground for steelhead trout and one can often see people fishing in the tree-shaded creek. But humans are not the only fishers here. Watch the big rocks in the creek bed and you may see an American Dipper. This small, plump, dark gray bird has distinctive flashing white eyelids. It bobs on the rocks, and then dives into the creek, where it can walk underwater or swim in search of insects, aquatic invertebrates, and fish fry. Wood Ducks also like the creek. American Crows find plenty of food in the forest, as do Scrub-Jays and the less common Gray Jays. One camper observed a flock of Cedar Waxwings descending like black-masked bandits on his dog food.

Elk and deer are quite common, and there are also chipmunks and other small mammals. Under the canopy of red alder, bigleaf maple, and Douglas-fir, look for vine maple, bracken fern, and sword fern. Also notice the baldhip roses. Their hips, or fruits, are orange or scarlet, and since the crown of sepals falls away early, the end of the hip is uniquely bald. Large false Solomon's seal is everywhere. This plant has big parallel-veined leaves alternating along the stem, which terminates in a thick show of white blossoms.

By the end of August, there is an abundance of edible berries in the forest; blue elderberries, blackberries, and thimbleberries all have sweet, tasty fruit. The Oregon-grape, too, was eaten by Native Americans, but because it is sour, was mixed with other fruit. Smaller plants include wild lettuce (a European import common in Douglas-fir forests), duckfoot, and vanillaleaf with its three big fan-shaped leaves and spikes of tiny white flowers. The dried leaves give out a vanilla scent and were used by some Native Americans as an insect repellent.

Directions: Gales Creek Campground is in the Tillamook State Forest, 17 miles from Forest Grove. Take US 26 west to Exit 53. On Oregon 6 (Wilson River Highway) watch for the Oregon State Forest campground sign on the right near milepost 35. Campground is open May to October only. Call State Forestry Office in Forest Grove (503-357-2191) to confirm exact dates. Entry fee.

Large false Solomon's seal.
Photo by Susan Peter

Amenities:

4 BLODGETT ARBORETUM

The John W. Blodgett Arboretum is a 45-acre preserve owned by Pacific University but open to members of the public. The two-mile main trail loops past Gales Creek and from December through April, steelhead spawn here. Kingfishers and American Dippers dive for smaller fish. Look down the high, steep bank of the creek and notice the dainty leaves and fine black stems of the five-fingered maidenhair fern. This fern requires a consistent supply of moisture and is usually found near waterfalls and splashy streams.

American Dippers.
Photo by Jim Cruce

Birds call from the bushes. Listen for the Chestnut-backed Chickadee, Dark-eyed Junco, and Song Sparrow. The Pileated Woodpecker can be heard tapping tree bark for insects. Both Ruffed and Blue grouse have been seen in the Arboretum.

Grand fir, Douglas-fir, western hemlock, and red-cedar create a deeply shaded forest with a rich carpet of meadow-rue, duckfoot, ferns, waterleaf, and salal, but showier wildflowers such as queen's cups (bead lilies), fawn lilies, bleeding-hearts, windflowers, and tiny pink starflowers are the true glories of the preserve. Persistent searchers may find at least four native orchids. The fairy slipper orchid has a showy, fragrant, bright pink blossom as much as an inch in diameter. This orchid is so fragile, that just picking the blossom will kill this endangered plant. All orchids are protected by law; do not touch. Coral-root comes in striped and spotted species; its tiny pinkish-brown to reddish-purple flowers grow in loose terminal clusters above long, thin brownish stems. The twayblade's name refers to the two small leaves about halfway down the hairy stem. Its flowers are very tiny (5 mm.) and pale green to yellowish in color. Rattlesnake plantain is another orchid, although it may at first glance be mistaken for English plantain. Look for a basal rosette of dark leaves with white mottling that follows the larger veins and a spike of numerous small waxy white flowers.

Directions: Take US 26 west to Exit 53. On Oregon 6, travel 13 miles, passing through Glenwood. Near milepost 38, 1.3 miles past the Timber turnoff, turn right onto Agaard Road and park. One trail access is directly across the highway; another is east of here a few hundred feet.

Amenities:

Rippling Waters is one of the few public access points to Gales Creek, home of the last best run of native steelhead trout in the Tualatin Basin. The oak, cottonwood, and red alder groves form a canopy over snowberry, reed canarygrass, sword fern, and red-osier dogwood. There are buttercups and several kinds of saxifrage underfoot, including the intriguing little piggy-back plant, which has a tiny bud from which a new plant develops right at the base of the heart-shaped leaf.

Himalayan blackberry is predominant in areas of this park. This aggressive exotic sprawls over the trails, crowding out a variety of native species. Nevertheless, birds enjoy the fruit and you may see American Robins, Song Sparrows, and chickadees as well as various warblers during spring migration. Take the trail down to Gales Creek. This area has been a popular swimming hole in the summer when the reduced volume of water makes the current less risky. Great Blue Herons and Common Mergansers still fish here. Check before you wet your line; current regulations require "catch and release."

Once an actively maintained park, it now needs a cooperative spirit between like-minded neighbors and volunteers to restore the trails. (If you're interested, consider contacting Larry Eisenberg, 503-846-4474, at Washington County Support Services.) The county is trying to discourage vandalism and dumping by eliminating parking at the entrance. Please park on one of the nearby side roads and expect to fight the brush a bit to get to the creek. The creek is about 100 yards from the highway.

Directions: On Gales Creek Road (Hwy. 8) 4.5 miles northwest of Forest Grove. The park is 0.2 miles past David Hill Road and just before you get to Roderick Creek Road. No sign is visible from the road, and only a wide gravel shoulder marks the site.

Female Common
Merganser.
Photo by Jim Cruce

6 RODGERS PARK

Though this seems to be a typical city park without much wildlife to note, it hosts a very special population well worth the stop. This great grove of Oregon white oaks hosts one of the two northernmost colonies of Acorn Woodpeckers in America. (The other colony is in the Columbia River Gorge.) The Acorn Woodpeckers seen at Pacific University, a few blocks away, are part of this colony. Novice birdwatchers are encouraged to seek out this pretty little bird; it is not too hard to spot, and being a late riser, is often still active even at midday.

The Acorn Woodpecker maintains a unique "larder" or granary. It makes small holes in the bark of selected trees, and into each hole pops an acorn ready for a winter meal. Look for a woodpecker with black back and tail, white sides and rump, and a little dark red cap on the very top of its head. It may be clinging to a trunk as much as 30 to 40 feet up, bobbing its head and upper body into a hole in the decaying wood of a snag or sawn-off vertical arching branch. Or you may recognize it in the air by the white spots on the underside of its wings. One favored tree is just west of the center of the park, about halfway to the sidewalk.

The City of Forest Grove has gone to some trouble to plant a variety of other trees in the park. There is a very large juniper — look for the berries. Some Native Americans used juniper berries to ease childbirth. Notice the fine Pacific yew with their reddish, flaky bark. The Atfalati thought the yew made the finest bows. So did the medieval English. Recently, taxol, a product of Pacific yew bark, provided a breakthrough treatment against some types of cancer. Taxol is now produced synthetically, sparing these native trees.

The prickly balls of seed hang onto the sweet gum even in the winter. This pretty tree, a native of the eastern U. S., is prized for its star-shaped leaves which turn bright crimson in the fall. And look up; squirrels also live in this park. Consider bringing a lawn chair or blanket so you can relax while watching the action in the treetops.

Directions:
From Highway 8 in Forest Grove, turn south on Elm Street. The park is at Elm and 18th.

Amenities:

Acorn Woodpecker.
*Above photo by
Michael Wilhelm*

AREA 1: Upper Tualatin River

7 FERNHILL WETLANDS

The utter tranquility of Fernhill Wetlands is a deception. This is a very busy place with a plethora of birds, fish, and insects dependent on the marsh environment. According to ecologist Rob Stockhouse, over 128 different species of wildflowers, grasses, sedges, and rushes as well as a variety of aquatic plants anchor the ecosystem here. Even wapato, something of a rarity locally, can be found here.

In August you may find young Ring-necked Pheasants or perhaps a Green Heron darting out from the sedges. Red-winged Blackbirds perch on small willows here, and pink-footed Glaucous-winged Gulls enjoy the water. Beside the one-mile path that loops around the lake, Queen Anne's lace provides a background for bright blue chicory blossoms. Like many Eurasian native plants brought to the New World as herb garden medicinals, these two now thrive as weeds. Chicory has also been used as a coffee substitute.

There is a small pond a short way up the road to the left. You may see a Great Blue Heron fishing in the shallows. A grove of tall Oregon ash stands sentinel over a tangled undergrowth of blackberry and wild rose. Listen carefully for the musical "maids-maids-maids! put on your tea — kettle-ettle-ettle" of the Song Sparrow.

Return to the main trail. Again, listen. There are crickets in the long grass, and watch for American Goldfinches in the patch of thistles just past the valve gates. Marsh Wrens like it here, as do Common Yellowthroats; the males have a black "bandit's mask." With their "wichety-wichety"song, these birds are more often heard than seen.

Overhead flies a skein of Canada Geese. Their honking calls are familiar to most Oregonians, but we are less likely to recognize the loud, high rattle made by the Belted Kingfisher as it hovers on rapidly beating wings ready to plunge after a fish. And there are plenty of fish to be seen leaping high out of the waters.

The Pied-billed Grebe, a small, brown diving bird, frequents the marsh year-round; it is the only grebe that regularly winters here. There are also flocks of Wood Ducks, Mallards, Green-winged Teals, and dowitchers. In fact, the 30 species of birds we identified on our early morning visit was typical for this lush, green ecosystem. Fernhill Wetlands is an area to return to again and again — each time the scene will be different as the season rings its changes.

Directions: From Highway 8 in Forest Grove go south on Highway 47. Left on Fern Hill Road.

Amenities:

Queen Anne's lace.
Photo by Susan Peter

This 20-mile-long state park was developed with help from "Rails to Trails," a national organization working to convert unused railway rights-of-way into public paths for biking, hiking, and horseback riding. Over half of this park is in the Tualatin Basin. It runs along the West Fork of Dairy Creek, and Mendenhall, Williams, and Brooke creeks. On the other side of the summit, the trail parallels Beaver Creek, a tributary of the Nehalem River.

You may access the trail off Highway 47 a mile north of Banks. This is an unmarked access with no place for parking. At the Vernonia, Tophill, and Buxton trailheads there are restrooms and the trail is accessible to hikers, bicycles, and horses. Low-gradient paved sections between Banks and Pongratz Road and the six-mile stretch south of Vernonia are suitable for wheelchairs.

From north of Banks, the trail runs through farmland and forestland. The vegetation shows the impact of human activity yet is surprisingly diverse. In the Banks area, the most prominent tree species are bigleaf maple and red alder, with a few Oregon ash and Douglas-fir. *continued* ➢

A view from the Shorebird Marsh at Fernhill Wetlands. *Photo by Brian Wegener*

Barn Owl. *Photo by Jim Cruce*

AREA 1: Upper Tualatin River

These trees are generally small, but do provide a shaded canopy over much of the trail. Understory plants include hazel, oceanspray, salal, and ferns. Weedy species such as Scotch broom, teasel, and stinging nettle are common. As the trail approaches the summit, it goes through a plantation of Douglas-fir.

You may see fox, deer, and elk along the trail, as well as owls in the woods and Great Blue Heron in the creeks. Park Ranger Scott Green says that the best wildlife viewing is in the unpaved seven-mile stretch from Buxton to Tophill, where he has seen coyote, bobcat, cougar, Blue Grouse, and Wild Turkey. Black-tailed deer are common around Mendenhall Creek, just north of the Buxton Trailhead.

Watch for the American Kestrel, previously called a sparrow hawk. This small hawk has a reddish tail or back and a handsome black and white face pattern. It can be seen hovering over a field on rapidly beating wings or sitting erect on poles, posts, or wires. Listen for Killdeer: you may hear its noisy cry before you spot this brown-backed, white-breasted bird with its distinctive double breast-rings and long rusty tail. American Crows form large flocks. The feathers, feet, and beak of this bird are all completely black and it flies with steady flapping, wings bent upwards. Its cousin, the Common Raven, is a much bigger bird, also all black, but with shaggy throat feathers and a heavier bill. The raven alternates flapping and soaring on flat wings.

Cutthroat trout can be found in Mendenhall Creek when the water is high. Dairy Creek and Beaver Creek have a winter run of steelhead trout.

Directions: The best access in the Tualatin watershed is at Buxton. Go west on Highway 26 to milepost 46. Turn right on Fisher Road and go north through Buxton. At Schmidlin Lane bear right and continue on Bacona Road to the Buxton trailhead. This is a total of 1.4 miles from the highway.

Amenities:

American Kestrel with prey on mullein.
Photo by Jim Cruce

Coyote. *Photo by Jim Cruce*

American Bittern in knotweed.
Photo by Jim Cruce

AREA 1: Upper Tualatin River

A marsh symphony awaits you at the junction of Sadd and Park Farms creeks. Willow leaves hiss as the wind cuts through them, the grasses and sedges rustle with anticipation, and the bird songfest swells into an overture.

If you stop by in the spring, you will hear courting rails, bitterns, wrens, and blackbirds. All nest in dense emergent vegetation. Sora and Virginia Rails are more often heard than seen. The secretive Sora emits a musical, descending whinny and a loud, whistled "pareet." The less common Virginia Rail renders a metallic "kidick, kidick," and a series of mallard-like quacks falling in pitch.

The hollow croaking of the American Bittern sounds like a water pump, "oonck-a-tsoonck." Skulking bitterns often freeze motionless in dense vegetation, with heads pointed towards the sun.

The restless long-billed Marsh Wren is another sun-worshipper as, with tail cocked upwards, it clings to bobbing cat-tails, sedges, and tall grass. This wren belts out explosive rattles, belying its small size. In the cat-tails, the scolding "kong-kareeee" of the Red-winged Blackbird is as distinctive as its crimson shoulder patch. Several kinds of swallows twitter and buzz amid hawk-shrieks and crow-laughter. There are moments when all the notes seem perfectly distinct, yet blend with the harmony of the singing marsh.

Directions: From the intersection of Highways 6 and 47 in Banks, take Highway 6 west 3.3 miles to milepost 46. Turn north on Cedar Canyon Road. Go 0.3 mile to the Y-intersection with Narup Road. Turn right (stay on Cedar Canyon Road). Go one mile east to the marsh, just beyond Killin Road. Park on Killin Road.

Amenities: Only the music! Please respect private property. View the birds and listen to the marshland fugue from the edge of the road. Only beavers and muskrats are allowed in the orchestra pit.

10   U. J. HAMBY PARK

This is a pretty little park close to downtown Hillsboro. While considerable impact from human activity must be expected, Hamby Park nevertheless accommodates a surprising variety of habitats and it is possible to see a number of both songbirds and waterfowl. The east end has a playground, bridges, native plantings around a pond, and wide asphalt paths. On the north edge of the lawn there is a long arc of lodgepole pines; note their two-needle leaf bundles. Along the ravine are several small blue spruce, natives of Colorado, and a pair of young sequoias from the Sierra Nevada of California. (South of the County Courthouse in Hillsboro are five of these *Sequoiadendron giganteum* planted in 1880.)

At the west end of the lawns, unpaved trails lead off into the woods and along the stream, a tributary of McKay Creek. Most of the many large trees here are western red-cedars. A system of natural trails runs through a half-mile of forest to the slough at Glencoe Road. The large number of stumps and logs is an unexpected feature of this suburban forest. Notice the amount of decay as one indication of how long ago these trees were cut. In a nurse log by the trail, several young trees have sprouted: a 12-foot red-cedar, a 6-inch Douglas-fir, and a 12-inch oak. Red huckleberry also roots this way and, down the trail, you'll find one sharing a stump with a vine maple and an Oregon-grape. This is the spot to look for Bewick's Wrens, Dark-eyed Juncos, Song Sparrows, and Black-capped Chickadees. Scrub-Jays call from the treetops.

It might be easier to catalog which native plants are not to be found here than to list those that are. This woodland-wetland has a large inventory of species including little pink starflowers, stinging nettles, Pacific yews, and Pacific dogwoods. Many small animals make their homes in this rich environment. By the water's edge you can find opossum and raccoon tracks.

Directions: Take US 26 to Jackson School Road exit. Travel two miles south to the light at Evergreen Road. Turn right, then left onto Jackson School Road again. The park is a mile farther on your right. Just after Arrington Road, turn right into the parking lot at Calvary Lutheran Church.

Amenities:

Vine maple.
Above photo by Susan Peter

Nurse Logs

By Susan Peter,
Geographer

Dead wood is a long-standing metaphor for anything burdensome or superfluous, indicating the need for removal or even destruction. These days, however, biologists routinely gather for Dead Wood Ecology and Management Symposiums.

These two facts illustrate one of the great misunderstandings about forest ecology. Standing snags, old stumps, and fallen logs are typically crawling with insects, oozy with slimy stuff, or riddled with nesting holes. This gives the impression that they harbor disease and that their death was maybe even the result of the life forms found in them after death. Slash burning was once considered the cure — remove the dead wood; improve the forest.

Now we know that this dead wood holds much of the secret of life for a forest and its inhabitants. Northern Spotted Owls are infamous for requiring snags for their nesting holes; they cannot survive without the "dead" upright trees. Some fish require woody debris in the stream for shelter and particular nutrients. And decaying logs and stumps are the nurseries where certain plants sprout and survive because of the special conditions found only there.

These nurse logs and stumps maintain water reservoirs in their spongy decaying texture. They also hold concentrated nutrients collected by the tree during its lifetime, plus the nutrients brought in by animal residents. In addition, a falling tree creates a hole in the forest canopy, allowing the light needed to encourage particular seedlings. Red-cedar, western hemlock, and Sitka spruce all often depend on nurse logs for regeneration. Sitka spruce, which grow all along our Pacific Northwest coast, are famous for their exposed roots, and are often seen stilted high above the soil after the stump which gave them life has rotted away. Red huckleberry and salal are other species which benefit from nurse logs, though the results are not so dramatic.

The next time you see a stump, see what you can find living on it. Watch for little trees growing from logs. Consider that some larger trees may seem to be growing in a line because, once upon a time, they shared the same nurse log. A few sites in this guide where you can be sure to find nurse logs include U. J. Hamby Park, Blodgett Arboretum, Summer Lake Park, Woods Memorial Park, Jordan Park, Tualatin Hills Nature Park, and PCC Rock Creek Nature Preserve.

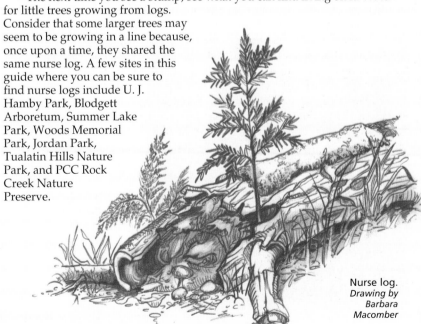

Nurse log.
*Drawing by
Barbara
Macomber*

11 GLENCOE SWALE

Behind Glencoe High School, McKay Creek has created a long wetland that includes ponds and sloughs. There are no established trails, but the local children scamper down the banks to explore and enjoy the diversity of wildlife. Some of these ponds have been created by beaver dams, and the builders are still in residence. Frogs enjoy this habitat as do crawfish, cutthroat trout, and leeches.

Both Red-tailed Hawks and Turkey Vultures sail in the sky in the spring and summer. The Red-tailed Hawk eats rats, squirrels, mice, rabbits, reptiles, and occasionally birds. The tail of a mature adult glows rusty red in sunlight. The Turkey Vulture, a scavenger that lives on carrion, is larger with great two-toned blackish wings that form a shallow "V "while in flight.

In the waters Great Blue Herons stand motionless, on the lookout for fish. There are deer in the woods and you may find their hoofprints. Look also for garter, blue racer, and rubber boa snakes. The rubber boa is one of only two boa snakes found in the U. S. and is quite common here in the Northwest. This burrowing snake has a shiny, brown skin that looks like rubber and its tail is a rounded snub, mimicking its head-end. Like all boas, it gives birth to live young and is a constrictor. That is, it kills by using the coils of its body to squeeze its prey to death and then swallows it whole. The boa's jaws can stretch to swallow animals larger than its head and it can then take several weeks to digest its food. But don't worry about your pet pooch — our local constrictor is rarely over a foot long and must limit itself to mice and such.

Directions:
From Oregon 8 in downtown Hillsboro, go north on 1st Avenue. Just after the road crosses McKay Creek slough, turn right onto Shannon Street. For a quieter view, follow Shannon uphill and turn left at 2nd Place (a cul-de-sac), or access from Glencoe High School grounds.

A Great Blue Heron enjoys a frog.
Photo by Jim Cruce

JACKSON BOTTOM WETLAND PRESERVE

If you visit this 650-acre preserve, your experience will vary greatly depending on the time of the year. In winter it boasts thousands of migratory waterfowl. The most common include Canada Geese, Mallard and Northern Pintail ducks, coots, cormorants, and Tundra Swans. Two covered viewing sites are accessible year round. In spring, summer, and fall you can explore 2.5 miles of trails, through marshes, forested wetlands, ponds, and along the Tualatin River, but from late November through April the trails are usually underwater.

Spring highlights include observing Great Blue Herons in a rookery on the eastern edge of the preserve and finding wildflowers and animal tracks in the woods. The Kingfisher Trail runs along the river, where you might see colorful Wood Ducks or Green Heron. On this trail in the summer you are likely to see or hear Song Sparrows and Common Yellowthroats.

Resident mammals include river otters, raccoons, beavers, nutria, and mink. Birds commonly seen here are Belted Kingfishers, Great Blue Herons, and Great Egrets. There is also a resident pair of Bald Eagles. Look for their nest high in the trees to the east. Great Horned Owls are also seen here regularly. Come here to see hawks, Marsh Wrens, four species of swallows, and maybe even the elusive American Bittern. In short, there is a tremendous variety of birds at Jackson Bottom throughout the year. Volunteers do a monthly bird survey in addition to working on a wide variety of habitat enhancement projects.

During the summer, you are sure to notice the plants that are such an important part of this habitat. You'll see that the reed canarygrass, an invasive pest, dominates much of the landscape. Look for low-growing waterpepper

continued ➤

A Double-crested Cormorant dries out its wings.
Photo by Jim Cruce

Cormorant with catch.
Photo by Michael WIlhelm

on the pond shorelines. This native knotweed is one of many species planted to help discourage the tall grass and increase diversity here. Also look for two special herbaceous perennials: wapato and poison hemlock. Wapato, once a staple of the Atfalati Indians but now uncommon, grows from a tuber. It has small white three-petaled flowers and long arrowhead-shaped leaves. You may need the help of one of the staff naturalists to find it. By contrast, poison hemlock, a member of the Parsley Family with purple splotches on its stems, grows in thick stands that are eight feet tall by the end of summer.

Jackson Bottom staff lead classes, tours, and field programs for hundreds of visitors annually. School groups come to learn about biodiversity, sensory awareness, and scientific inquiry, and to conduct steward-ship projects. Families can take a night hike and go on a bird walk, or even a canoe tour. Hands-on learning is the staff's specialty and getting dirty is strongly encouraged.

Directions: From Oregon 8 in Hillsboro, go south on First Avenue (Hwy. 219) to the edge of town. The north viewing shelter is on the left adjacent to the old water treatment plant at the edge of the slough. One half mile farther, also on the left side of the highway, is the main entrance with plenty of parking and the Kingfisher Marsh Trailhead.

Amenities:

Wapato.
*Drawing by
Barbara Macomber*

The Atfalati

By Shirley Ewart,
Anthropologist

The first white explorers who came into the Tualatin River Valley were entranced by the park-like meadows dotted with oak groves and saw these grasslands as future farm sites ready for the plough. What they did not know was that this was an artificial landscape, a carefully managed ecosystem maintained on a vast scale for hundreds of years by the people who had lived in the area for possibly 10,000 years.

The Atfalati, also called the Tualaty, lived throughout the Tualatin River Basin. They, like many other people in the Willamette Valley, spoke the Kalapuyan language. "Kalapuya" means "long grass" and it was the long grass of the open meadows that dominated their landscape and was the ideal habitat for camas, tarweed, deer, and elk.

To preserve the long grass environment and to assure the survival of the plants and animals essential to their diet and their culture, the Atfalati used fire on a massive scale. By setting fire to the land every fall, they discouraged underbrush and young trees. At this time of the year, the camas had been harvested; its bulbs and the buds of next spring's grass were underground and protected from the fire. Then, in the late fall, fresh new grass became available for geese, swans, ducks, and other fowl as well as for deer and elk.

Burning also improved acorn production. Fire had little effect on mature oak trees, but it prevented them from forming extensive, thick canopied forests in the valley. Without competition from other trees, the oaks produced more acorns, and burning the grass cover made the fallen nuts easier to gather. The fire also was essential for the tarweed harvest. Burning the grass left the tarweed standing but burned off the sticky "tar" so the seeds could be easily harvested.

At the ecotone, the point where two ecosystems converge, the most diverse biological populations develop because plants and animals native to both ecosystems can be sustained. Along the creeks and rivers where prairie and forest intersect, water is plentiful and woody shrubs provide deer browse. The Atfalati kept this area free from fire to support and concentrate the deer herds, which made hunting easier.

During the winter, the Atfalati lived in longhouses in settled villages. Some of these were near present-day Hillsboro, Beaverton, Forest Grove, along lower Scoggins Creek, and near Gaston. In the spring, small groups moved out to take advantage of the available resources, building brush shelters if they needed them, or living in the open.

The Atfalati depended mainly on plant food, less on game, and hardly at all on fish. The principal carbohydrates were camas, wapato, and tarweed seeds. They roasted camas bulbs in pit ovens and then pounded and molded the pulp into thick cakes that could be stored. The women dug wapato from the muddy wetlands, and boiled or roasted the roots. They ground the tarweed seeds to make a flour, or mixed the seeds with cooked camas and hazelnuts. Sunflower seeds were also ground and eaten; the stalks were eaten raw. Women and children picked summer fruits to eat fresh. In the late summer they dried berries on bark trays set near the fire. Hazelnuts were picked green, beaten to take off the husks, sunbaked, shelled, and stored. Before the Atfalati could grind acorns into flour, they had to leach out the bitter tannin by soaking the nuts in water or burying them in damp mud. They used a number of different plants for teas. Tobacco was grown from seeds sown in wood ash; this was the only agriculture the Atfalati practiced.

Hunting provided the Atfalati with deer and elk meat which they ate broiled or smoked and dried. They ate rabbits, squirrels, and raccoons as well as ducks, geese, swans, and grouse. They did not eat lizards, snakes, foxes, coyotes, bears, or birds of prey.

Fish was not very important to the Atfalati, but they caught eels at night by the light of pitch brands. Hooks and lines were used for trout fishing and suckers were often caught bare-handed. They enjoyed mussels, if available, and used the shells for spoons and scrapers. At Oregon City, the powerful Chinook controlled the salmon fishing and the Atfalati traded for salmon, bringing wapato, deer meat, camas, and slaves (which they got by raiding other groups). The Chinook at the falls did allow the Atfalati to catch lamprey eels.

Atfalati technology depended on stone, wood, animal bone and hides, and plant fiber. Stone was the most important material because without good quality stone, it would have been impossible to prepare trees for housing, or to make tool handles or bone awls and needles. Hammers, fishing weights, and mortars and pestles to grind seeds and nuts into meal, were all made out of stone. To cook food, they heated round stones in the fire and then dropped them into bark baskets holding soup or stew. Obsidian, obtained in trade, was the most prized stone. Fine arrow points could be made from this volcanic glass, but most Atfalati hunters had to settle for flint or, to kill small game, hardwood points.

Wood furnished tool handles and weapons. The Atfalati made their bows of Pacific yew or oak; some were six feet in length and it is thought that perhaps they were used horizontally. Arrows were made from the shoots of oceanspray bushes. Each arrow had three feathers and both these and the arrow points were lashed to the shaft with pitch-glued sinew. Only war arrows were poison-tipped, and rattlesnake venom was used for this purpose.

Oregon ash was used for trays for food preparation and service, and the dried bark was useful for plugging holes in house walls. Service berry wood made good, tough digging sticks and willow wood was used for plates and fire drills. The red-cedar was important. It furnished planks for houses, as well as bark, which could be beaten, frayed, and fashioned into women's dresses. The Atfalati made canoes 14 to 30 feet long. They hollowed out whole trunks of red-cedar, cottonwood, or white pine and made paddles out of maple. Fishing lines and rope were braided from hazel and willow fiber and also from the fibrous stems of stinging nettles. Cow parsnip stalks became deer callers and flutes. The Atfalati women made baskets from willow and hazel shoots. They used fluff from cat-tail heads to stuff the buckskin padding in their babies' cradles.

The men made fishhooks, scrapers, awls, and needles from animal bones. The women tanned the hides of deer, elk, mountain lion, lynx, beaver, and gray fox for blankets. They cut rabbit and squirrel hides into strips and wove them to make cloaks. Rich people might wear blankets woven from wild cat skin. Poor people just tied a deer skin around their bodies. The men's distinctive caps were made from small animal furs complete with ears. Otter was trapped and the soft fur used for shaman's ceremonial belts and to bind braided hair. On ceremonial occasions, eagle feathers and woodpecker scalps were displayed and worn.

Thus the Atfalati maintained themselves successfully for thousands of years until their ultimate doom by European diseases, the collapse of the fur trade, and the influx of settlers into Oregon. In 1782-83 smallpox ravaged the Native American populations of Oregon. Venereal diseases, such as syphilis, were introduced in the 1790s and malaria between 1830 and 1833. It was estimated that nearly 70 percent of the Kalapuya died during these years.

These illnesses affected the able bodied as well as children and the old; people who are seriously ill cannot hunt, dig, or gather and must be cared for by others.

The collapse of the fur trade also hurt the Kalapuyan peoples. Both the Pacific Fur Company and the Hudson's Bay Company accepted beaver skins in exchange for wool blankets and metal knives and implements. In the 19th century, European fashion changed and the gentry preferred silk hats to the tall beaver felt hats. By then, Native Americans were ill equipped to go back to using stone tools and furs for clothing and blankets.

Finally, the influx of white settlers into Oregon was the death knell for the Indians. After 1850, the Donation Land Act sparked an enormous rush to the Pacific Northwest. The Atfalati were promised that the U. S. Government would pay for the land that the white settlers had seized and fenced, but no payment was ever made. The pioneers' cattle could not be considered "game," and yet competed with the deer and elk for grass. Their pigs rooted up the camas bulbs. More seriously, the newcomers, when they occupied a piece of land, considered it their own private property and did not want Indians wandering around or hunting on that property. They certainly did not want the grasslands fired. They did not mind the Indians living in the winter villages, as long as the land around those villages was considered surplus to the farmers' needs. When hungry Native Americans raided the settlers' farmsteads, the settlers caught and whipped them.

By 1851, the 1,000 to 2,000 Atfalati reported in 1780 had dwindled to just 65. This exhausted remnant signed a treaty with the U. S. Government which promised that they would be given their own land including Wapato Lake. Unfortunately, the United States Senate never ratified this treaty. For the next four years the Atfalati resisted the U. S. Government's intention to relocate them east of the Cascades. In 1855, the government decided that the Atfalati would go to the reservation at Grand Ronde and the very small remaining group signed a new document. By 1890, there were only 28 Atfalati left. The last speaker of the Atfalati language died in 1928.

Today, little of the Atfalati heritage remains. The name, changed to "Tualatin," remains as the name of our river. Most recently, through the efforts of the Tualatin Riverkeepers, a 40-foot waterfall has been named in honor of Ki-A-Kuts, the last Atfalati chief. In museums and in private collections we may find pestles and mortars, fishhooks, and arrowheads. Early anthropologists documented the Atfalati way of life and translated Atfalati legends and stories.

Perhaps the most important thing that the Atfalati have left us is a lesson. To the Atfalati, everything, including the plants and animals used for food, had a spirit which was dangerous to upset. Proper respect meant using the land and its resources with care for each living thing. Thus the land supported the people and, for thousands of years, the people survived. Can we learn to tread as carefully?

Cougar.
Photo by Jim Cruce

VIEWING AREA 2: Rock Creek

Viewing Sites

1. Rock Creek Nature Preserve/PCC
2. Emerald Estates Park
3. Bethany Lake Park
4. Amberglen Wetland
5. Noble Woods Park
6. Century High School Wetlands
7. Little Park on Reedville Creek
8. Hillwood Park
9. Turner Creek Park
10. Rood Bridge Road Park

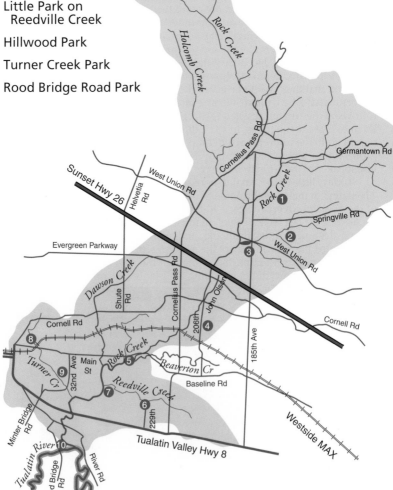

VIEWING AREA 2: Rock Creek

Western yellow pond-lily. *Photo by Susan Peter*

Rock Creek drains many miles of the Skyline Boulevard ridge with its major upper tributaries coming together in the lowland along the far north end of 185th Avenue (between Springville and Germantown roads). A lesser tributary, from the east, joins at Bethany Lake. Rock Creek then flows through the country club that borrows its name and continues in fine style under Sunset Highway, which bridges both the stream and the paved bicycle path that parallels it. South of the freeway, an undeveloped greenway buffers Rock Creek from the many changes taking place throughout east Hillsboro. Beaverton Creek, coming from the east, doubles the size of Rock Creek, then Dawson Creek comes in from the north near the airport. Two more small creeks, Reedville (from the flatlands west of Aloha) and Turner (passing through older east Hillsboro neighborhoods), join in just before Rock Creek crosses under Tualatin Valley Highway (Hwy. 8). South of the highway, it passes the sewage treatment plant and flows along the edge of Rood Bridge Road Park. There it joins the Tualatin River.

Bethany Lake Park (see page 29).
Photo by Brian Wegener

BETHANY
LAKE PARK
TUALATIN HILLS PARK
& RECREATION DISTRICT

Rock Creek Nature Preserve is managed by PCC's Rock Creek Environmental Studies Center. Before your trip, it is strongly suggested that you visit their website (http://spot.pcc.edu/rcesc/index.htm) for lists of the many plant and animal species in the preserve. These splendid acres of woodland and meadows are well worth a visit any time of the year, but especially in early May when the camas is in bloom.

Unpaved trail: (two miles round trip) As soon as you step under the trees, you feel as if you are deep in the woods, and other than evidence of long-ago logging, these woods seem to be much as they were when the Atfalati hunted here nearly

Northern Flicker.
Photo by Jim Cruce

200 years ago. Just inside the gate, notice the oceanspray bushes on both sides of the trail. In the summer, the long, white, foam-like clusters droop over the leaves. Later, the flowers fade, persisting as dry husks into the winter. The Atfalati used the straight young shoots for arrows.

Come into the forest of Douglas-fir, red-cedar, hemlock, and vine maple. In March, look for trilliums in the undergrowth. Even after the flowers have withered, it is easy to recognize the whorl of three big leaves. In May, you can find large false Solomon's seal, wood violets, and Oregon-grape. The slender stems of miniature (1 cm. blossoms) pink starflowers spring right out of their whorl of leaves. Tiger lilies have many sets of whorled leaves along their 2-foot-tall stems and flaunt flame-orange flowers in summer.

Look and listen. The signs of woodpecker activity are all around. Northern Flickers are abundant. The songs of Black-capped Chickadees and Red-breasted Nuthatches are heard throughout the woods. Look for Bewick's Wrens, Winter Wrens, Golden-crowned Kinglets, and Ruby-crowned Kinglets.

Exit by the gate, cross the old farm road, and go through the metal gate. Turn right. Notice the fringe-cups, a tall member of the Saxifrage Family. Its basal leaves are somewhat heart-shaped, and the greenish-white flowers with their fringe-tipped petals are very fragrant. After a short distance the trail becomes a raised boardwalk, and the woods

Starflower. *Photo by Susan Peter*

Small camas.
Photo by Susan Peter

give way to a large meadow. The rustling of grass betrays the presence of a garter snake and spiders scuttle over the planks. In the field to the left there is a stand of Oregon white oaks. The jewels of this lovely spot appear in early May. Beautiful blue camas flowers are sprinkled among the grass. Paul Kane, the Irish-Canadian artist who came to Oregon in 1846, remarked on the "most verdant and beautiful appearance" of these plants which he described as an "uninterrupted sheet of bright ultramarine blue." Camas roots provided a staple carbohydrate for the Native Americans. Stand still for a moment and again, look and listen. Maybe you hear a Red-winged Blackbird staking out his territory. Perhaps a Red-tailed Hawk soars overhead. At the end of the boardwalk, you will want to retrace your steps.

Paved trail: (one mile round trip) The asphalt trail leads first past a little meadow. Beside the trail, it is hard to miss the patch of Scarlet Pimpernel with its numerous bright red flowers. This English import is called "the poor man's weather glass" in its native land because the flowers shut if rain is imminent.

After passing through a gate, notice the big service berry bush on your right. Sun-dappled log benches at each turn of the multi-looped trail make lovely resting places and offer a fine opportunity to admire the canopy of vine maples and large hazels and the understory of sword fern, wood violet, fringe-cups, and Oregon-grape. Look for mushrooms and huge shelf fungi. At the end of the trail, down some steps, is a gate which is usually locked; take a peek over it for a different view of the large meadow.

Directions: Highway 26 to Exit 64. North on 185th. Cross West Union Road and turn right on Springhill Road. PCC Rock Creek is on the left. Weekdays you will need to buy a $2 parking permit at the PCC entrance.
Unpaved trail: enters the woods at the northwest corner of Building 3.
Paved trail: is gated and enters the woods at the far northeast corner of Parking Lot A.
Note: The preserve is generally kept unlocked from early April to mid-November. Access at other times, or for groups of more than five, can be arranged by calling PCC (503-244-6111).

Amenities:

2 EMERALD ESTATES PARK

Praying mantis.
*Photo by
Monte Rumgay*

A narrow asphalt path between two houses leads to the top of a stairway. Enjoy this long view of a major Rock Creek tributary and the series of undeveloped parks along it, including this 14-acre jewel. Follow the dirt path under the power lines and look up. On the power line supports, birds of prey, such as American Kestrels and Sharp-shinned Hawks, perch and watch for their next meal. A mile or more of path wanders through meadowland, at one point passing a line of recently planted trees including cherries. In the summer, the meadow has tall grasses interspersed with Canada and bull thistles, Himalayan blackberries, and other such unwelcome weeds. Note the small fireweed with its minimal, slender leaves and simple, tiny, pale pink flowers. In the fall these, like the larger fireweed, will have long seedpods that split into curls to release their silky fluff.

These grassy areas are a good place to look for sparrows: Savannah Sparrows in the summer and Golden-crowned Sparrows in the winter. Song Sparrows are common year round. And, at the end of summer, expect to find American Goldfinches feeding on thistle seeds.

Full-grown ash and willow trees mark this branch of Rock Creek. This wooded area hosts a variety of forest birds: Northern Flickers, Black-capped Chickadees, Dark-eyed Juncos, Spotted Towhees, and Bewick's Wrens. Western Scrub-Jays, too, value this habitat, using both trees and the grassy areas. There is a side trail leading down to a plank bridge and residential areas north of the park. Look in the summertime grasses for praying mantis.

Golden-crowned Sparrows. *Photo by Michael Wilhelm*

Directions: From Hwy. 26, go north on 185th one mile to West Union Road. Take a right on West Union Road. Left on Laidlaw, left on Waterford to 16800 block. There is no sign at the park entrance.

Amenities:

3 BETHANY LAKE PARK

Birder Brian Wegener writes: "It may be a stretch to call the resident waterfowl 'wildlife'." Still, this pond, formed by a small dam on Rock Creek, has a variety of attractions. Begging you for handouts will be Canada Geese, domestic white geese, domesticated White-fronted Geese, and Mallards. You may also see some white swans with yellow-tipped orange beaks. These are old-world Mute Swans which are now locally naturalized in the United States. Our native Whistler and Trumpeter Swans have black beaks. Please resist the urge to feed these birds as Bethany Lake has problems with water quality. Nevertheless, there are sculpin and other small fry in these waters and Great Blue Herons stand silently watching for fish. There are also some cutthroat trout and a sign reminds anglers that, to be kept, these must be at least eight inches long.

Stop for a moment. Listen and look up. Song Sparrows provide music and Red-winged Blackbirds add their own cheery calls, while a Red-tailed Hawk wheels overhead.

In late summer, note the curly dock along the half-mile of trail. The entire plant has turned a deep reddish chocolate brown as it has gone to seed. This is also a good time and place to admire the luscious-looking wild rose hips. See how many wild rose varieties you can find. Spring is a good time to see that the water lilies growing here are actually native pond-lilies. Look for their compact, spherical bright yellow blooms; they were an important source of food for Native Americans in Oregon.

Follow the wide asphalt path to the west end of the lake. Below the small earthen dam, Oregon ash trees shade a bridge as Rock Creek turns south. The trail follows the creek for a little distance, and then ends in a residential neighborhood. The mowed lawn continues south, but the creek becomes inaccessible behind mountains of Himalayan blackberries.

Directions: From Highway 26 exit onto 185th Avenue. North on 185th Avenue for less than a mile. Just before the light at the West Union Road intersection, see power lines and a Tualatin Hills Park and Recreation District sign on the left. Park on wide shoulder either side of 185th.

Amenities:

Curly dock.
Photo by Susan Peter

④ AMBERGLEN WETLAND

Those familiar with Amberglen Corporate Park may be surprised to discover this small wild glade. Soft trails lead to tall Douglas-fir trees shading a bridge over a little tributary of Rock Creek. Duckweed, water-cress, *Veronica,* and knotweed grow beside tall cat-tails in the ponds formed by beaver dams. Look for Belted Kingfishers and listen for their distinctive "rattle" call. Watch for songbirds along other trails that lead through open grassy slopes.

There are several benches. Note the poison oak climbing up the Douglas-fir behind one of them. Poison oak has characteristic shiny lobed leaves in sets of three, but size, color, and growth habit vary considerably between individual plants. Learn to recognize it so you don't accidentally someday pick a fall bouquet of the beautiful red leaves!

Birder Brian Wegener suggests you travel a few blocks east to the large grassy park near the intersection of Von Neumann Drive and Amberglen Parkway. This he describes as "a very unnatural habitat that is loaded with waterfowl and gulls." Many of the birds here are exotic species of ducks and geese. There are some very peculiar hybrid ducks here, the result of interbreeding between Mallards and these domesticated species. In the winter, this pond hosts a large flock of American Wigeons; they may be seen both on the water and grazing on the lawn. Scan the flock very carefully and you may see a Eurasian Wigeon or two mixed in with the "baldpates" or American Wigeons. The Eurasian Wigeon has red-brown head with a buff crown. Look for the Lesser Scaup; the males have black heads and blue bills and the females sport a sharp white patch at the base of their bills. Pink-footed Glaucous-winged Gulls can also be spotted here.

Poison oak. *Photo by Susan Peter*

Directions: From Highway 26 take 185th Avenue exit south. Right at Evergreen Parkway. Left at John Olsen Avenue (aka 206th). South of Amberwood Drive, see the park on the left as the road dips. Park on a side street to your right. Barkdust trails lead from the street down to the stream. The MAX Quatama Station is half a mile south of the park, and there are good sidewalks.

Amenities:

The Belted Kingfisher
By Brian Wegener

Drawing by
Barbara
Macomber

Perched on a branch of a downed tree with a crawfish in its mouth, a Belted Kingfisher takes a rest before entering its nest in the bank of the Tualatin. The distinctive "rattle call" alerts you to its presence. Then suddenly the bird flies up and enters a hole in the steep, eroded river-bank. Within a minute it flies out of the nesting hole, and is off to hunt for small fish, crustaceans, or amphibians.

A quarter mile from the river and away from water, you might never see this amazing bird, but once you get through the riparian border of Oregon ash and red-osier (creek) dogwood, the Belted Kingfisher becomes a common species. A Belted Kingfisher is easy to identify: larger than a robin with a large crested head, stout but sharp three-inch bill, blue-gray coloration on the back and head with white under-neath, white around the throat with a blue-gray "belt" across the breast. A rust-colored band below this belt distinguishes the female. You will often see the bird flying low over the river or perched on an overhanging branch.

In June you can view Belted Kingfishers bringing food to their nestlings. After the banks of the Tualatin have eroded in winter floods, Belted Kingfishers and Northern Rough-winged Swallows excavate their nests. To locate kingfisher nests, look for four-inch diameter holes in the soil. On the bottom edge of the holes you will notice grooves made by the birds dragging their feet as they fly into the holes. The nesting cavities are usually three to six feet deep, sometimes up to 12 feet deep. The kingfishers will often perch on a nearby branch for a minute before entering the hole. While they are perching, you can study what is on the menu for lunch, drooping from both sides of the bird's bill.

Sometime in early June the nestlings will fledge. Both parents will hunt with their family of five to eight fledglings for about 10 days. The adults will drop dead or stunned food in the water for the young to learn to catch. In less than two weeks, when the young kingfishers are able to hunt on their own, they are excluded from the parents' feeding territory. You can sometimes map out the feeding territory of a kingfisher by following it in a canoe or kayak. The bird will keep ahead of you until you reach the edge of the territory, at which time it will turn around and fly back behind you. The same territory-mapping technique works with herons.

World-wide there are 87 species of kingfishers. The Belted Kingfisher is the most widespread of the three North American species. With riparian forests, small fish and crustaceans, and plenty of steeply eroded banks with soft soils, the Tualatin River provides ideal habitat for the Belted Kingfisher.

5 NOBLE WOODS PARK

Stepping stones across Rock Creek.
Photo by Susan Peter

Noble Woods Park straddles the bottomlands of Rock Creek with an upland forest of red-cedar, Douglas-fir, and bigleaf maple. The creek travels through swamps, groves of Oregon ash, and wide grassy meadowlands. Rock Creek is relatively large here because Beaverton Creek, with its own sizeable flow, joined it just a few feet east of the park boundary. Over a mile of wide solid paths loop through the forest across bridges and boardwalks to view points. One well-maintained side trail leads to ponds and stepping stones that cross the creek. Here you can see crawfish, small fish, and tiny white freshwater mussel shells on the creek's gravel bottom.

In this beautiful park you are likely to see small forest-dwelling birds like Black-capped Chickadees and Bewick's Wrens. The calls of Northern Flickers are commonly heard from high in the trees. Listen for a distinctive scream; a pair of Red-tailed Hawks has been seen in the treetops.

If you are visiting the park in the fall, this is a good place to identify plants through their berries. Red rose hips are common. These are a good source of vitamin C and can be made into jelly, but most of the other berries you see won't be edible. Look for the large, loose clusters of white berries on the red-osier dogwood bushes. The Pacific dogwood, with its showy white-bracketed blossoms, is less common and has bright red berries. Note, too, the tight groupings of three to six white berries on the small and relatively sparse snowberry bushes. These hang on through the winter and look like little tufts of snow caught in bare branches.

Ninebark is another large lowland shrub found here. It has a small palmate leaf and thick clusters of white blossoms strung along its branches in the spring; by August these have been converted to pale green seedpods with papery coverings. Also in August, look high up into the treetops for the pale green tassels of Oregon ash seeds. Each seed is attached to a little papery wing and waits for autumn winds to send it flying. The maples have winged seeds too, but are paired and less papery.

A vine well distributed along Tualatin Valley creeks is the European bittersweet nightshade, bearing fruit and flowers throughout summer. You'll spot its translucent oval blood-red berries hanging gracefully in loose array

6 CENTURY HIGH SCHOOL WETLANDS

A short woodsy path leads through a few tall Douglas-firs and an old overgrown filbert orchard to a ponded stretch of Reedville Creek. This is a good opportunity to see how nature reclaims untended farmland. How old are these Douglas-firs? At this elevation they can easily grow 25 feet tall in their first dozen years. At 30 years of age, their trunks can be more than a foot in diameter. Douglas-fir seeds easily around here. Look for their tiny two-inch seedlings where the ground is relatively bare and some sunlight can get in.

Douglas-fir is native only to the Pacific Northwest and is the most common tree in our evergreen forests. Its Latin name, *Pseudotsuga menziesii*, commemorates a Scot, Archibald Menzies, who identified it as a unique species in 1791. The common name honors another Scot, botanist David Douglas, who explored this region from 1825-1827. Notice how frequently Douglas' name shows up in the natural world.

Grass and thickets of willow and blackberry along the pond give good refuge for a pair of Mallards that nest here. You may also see Belted Kingfishers and at least one Great Blue Heron. Scrub-Jays and crows are noisy as they look for food. Peterson describes these birds as "omnivorous" and they certainly are, eating berries, insects, and "people food" with equal relish. Black-capped Chickadees and Bushtits balance on slender grasses to pick at the seeds, while gangs of Cedar Waxwings attack berries of all kinds. Birder Laura Hill reports that Yellowthroats, Yellow Warblers, and Wilson's Warblers have all been spotted here. These tiny, brightly colored birds are insect eaters. This great wetland habitat provides a fine ecological laboratory for the high school students. How fortunate that it has been preserved.

Directions: From Tualatin Valley Highway (Hwy. 8) turn north on 229th Avenue. This becomes 67th Avenue. Park where 67th ends at Blaine Street.

Amenities:

Cedar Waxwing in service berry.
Photo by Jim Cruce

Animal Tracks and the Stories They Tell
Whose Tracks Are These?

Story and drawings by Steve Engel

It's April in the Northwest. There is a patch of mud beneath ash and cottonwood along the Tualatin River in northwestern Oregon. Overhanging branches and leaves have directed recent raindrops onto a portion of it, leaving the other half smooth and unpocked. Hand-like feet are imprinted on its surface, clues to who has passed by not too long ago, for they are fresh and clear. **Whose tracks are here, along this slow meandering drainage?**

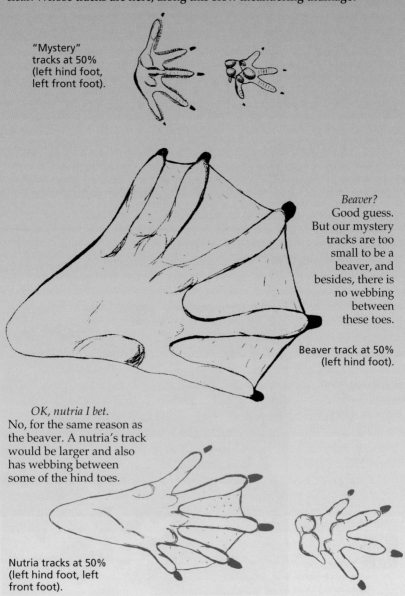

"Mystery" tracks at 50% (left hind foot, left front foot).

Beaver? Good guess. But our mystery tracks are too small to be a beaver, and besides, there is no webbing between these toes.

Beaver track at 50% (left hind foot).

OK, nutria I bet. No, for the same reason as the beaver. A nutria's track would be larger and also has webbing between some of the hind toes.

Nutria tracks at 50% (left hind foot, left front foot).

I need a hint.

Look closer. What can the tracks tell us? How big is the animal? How does it walk? Is it wide-bodied with short legs or is it narrow-bodied with long legs? Was it running? Was it scared, calm, hungry, alone? Which way was it going? What is over there that might interest it? Was it carrying anything? Dragging anything? What animals have four toes on some feet and five on the others? What animal would be at home here in this land of river, marsh and swamp?

Go down by the water. Who chewed those sedges? Who left six-inch-long stems of cat-tail cut like a knife at each end? Who left this soft round pellet of digested plant material? Who built that tiny lodge of grass and mud in the pond? Who swims in the water without webbing but with a fringe of stiff hair surrounding each hind toe? Look for its shadow on the five-toed prints. (Yes, that's right, the front feet are the four-toed ones.)

Who is trapped by the millions each winter for its coat and graces many a stew pot under the moniker of marsh rabbit? Who is actually a rodent? Who is your neighbor? Don't you know?

The tracks tell you: **Muskrat,** *Ondatra zibethica.*

These tracks were found along the Tualatin River at Jackson Bottom Wetlands, Hillsboro. Lowland areas throughout western Oregon are excellent places to look for tracks of wildlife in March and April. At this time of year, with subsiding high water and before grasses have begun to grow through the sand, silt and mud, tracking conditions are excellent and animal activity is high.

Steve Engel is a tracker, naturalist and educator living in Portland, Oregon.

Muskrat. *Photo by Jim Cruce*

Tracks You May Find

Here are some animal tracks you may find in the Tualatin River Basin.
See how many you can find.

Track samples by Steve Engel (not to scale).

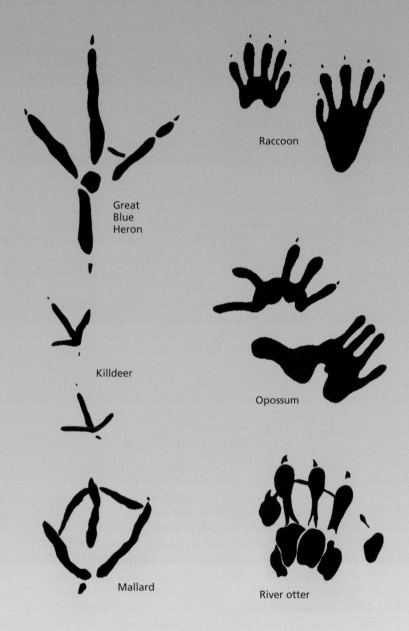

Raccoon

Great
Blue
Heron

Killdeer

Opossum

Mallard

River otter

7 LITTLE PARK ON REEDVILLE CREEK

A tiny patch of mowed meadow next to a babbling brook is shaded by a black hawthorn, some Oregon ash, and a small grove of young alders; this presents a very good riparian habitat for songbirds. Listen for chickadees and Song Sparrows and watch for the Red-breasted Nuthatch as it works its way headfirst down the tree trunk. Its high "enk enk" cry has been described as sounding like a tiny tin horn. Also, watch for flocks of gregarious little Bushtits as they move from bush to tree communicating in soft "t'sits."

In this very quiet little park, find common touch-me-not (jewelweed) along the water and a knee-high grass meadow beyond the mowed lawn. This is Reedville Creek before it disappears into a thicket just upstream of the swale where it joins Rock Creek. You can get a glance of this wetland north of the big bend on Brookwood Avenue if you continue north beyond the Golden Road turn-off.

Directions: From Tualatin Valley Highway (Hwy. 8), turn north on Brookwood, right on Golden Road, left on SE 51st Avenue. Park on the street where SE 51st Avenue dips down to cross Reedville Creek. On west side of street, a pale green electrical service box marks the top of dirt steps cut into the slope.

Red-breasted Nuthatch. *Photo by Jim Cruce*

8 HILLWOOD PARK

Access 1: A soft path leads you under some weeping willows to Turner Creek. Here, the creek forms a pond rimmed with grasses, sedges, and rushes. Young red-osier dogwood, alder, ash, and steeple bush with its spires of tiny, pink to deep rose flowers, have been planted; teasel and horsetail were already here. Himalayan blackberry prevents further exploration downstream, although this park continues between backyards for a quarter of a mile. You can expect to find common backyard songbirds like American Robins in this part of the park. And listen, that loud "keyeeeer" call from the treetops indicates the presence of a flicker.

Access 2: This is a much larger pond surrounded by more varied and mature greenery. There is no trail, but the slight elevation is useful. In the fall and winter, this is the place to look for waterfowl and wading birds. In the spring, take a look at the water's edge to see skunk cabbage. The bright yellow spathe surrounds a narrow, poker-like spike of tiny flowers. The big leaves can be up to five feet long and have a strong skunky smell. During the summer, notice the bittersweet nightshade with its purple flowers and long, deep yellow stamens projecting from the corolla. As summer turns to fall, the berries change from green, through yellow and orange, to a glowing bright red. Like those of many nightshades, these berries are poisonous. Another import is the large wild morning glory that drapes itself freely around the jewelweed and cat-tails.

Directions: Traveling westbound on Tualatin Valley Highway (Hwy. 8) the road curves right and becomes 10th Avenue in Hillsboro. Go north on 10th.
Access 1: 10th Avenue curves right and becomes Cornell Road. Turn right on Grant Street, right on NE 14th Avenue, right on Hillwood Drive to the 300 block. Park at the grassy meadow (no sign).
Access 2: From 10th Avenue turn right on Main Street, left onto NE 18th Avenue. To the left is a roadway between a pair of brick entry pillars. Turn in here. Viewing is from the gravel shoulder just before this becomes a private road.

Hillwood Park.
Photo by Susan Peter

Residents of Hillwood Park

Teasel. *Susan Peter*

Steeple bush (hardhack). *Susan Peter*

Cat-tail. *Susan Peter*

American Robin. *Jim Cruce*

Wood Ducks on house. *Michael Wilhelm*

Cardinal meadowhawk (dragonfly). *Steve Berliner*

9 TURNER CREEK PARK

Most of this 12-acre park is devoted to soccer and baseball fields, tennis courts, and a children's playground. In the wet season, notice that the soccer field hosts both Glaucous-winged and Ring-billed gulls. Follow the paved trail that loops around these and downhill towards a bench by Turner Creek. From there, unpaved trails continue to a bridge and skirt the shore of a pond before returning to the tennis courts. Across the bridge, a wooded trail leads to the W. L. Henry Elementary School.

You'll find jewelweed, *Veronica*, purple iris (flag), knotweed, and sedges growing on the edges of this lush, swampy pond which is full of tiny fish, frogs, and water skimmers. A pretty little yellow sunflower called nodding beggar-tick likes the water's edge, too. It has several 1.5-inch-diameter flowers to a stem and each has eight green sepals that curl back from the composite bloom. The name is descriptive; these flowers really do nod, especially after the seeds have formed, and microscopic hooks on the U-shaped seeds would surely have stuck to the rough clothes of tramps and other beggars. Typical of the Sunflower Family, you'll find them blooming in the summer and fall.

Red-winged Blackbirds are comfortable here, as are a variety of songbirds. Look for Great Blue Herons that fish along the creek. And watch out, don't step on the garter snake sunning itself on the gravel path.

Note: There is another access to Turner Creek on Camwel Street off SW 32nd. This has a fine red footbridge and lush forest, but the trail does not connect with the other trails in the park.

Directions: From Tualatin Valley Highway (Hwy. 8), turn north on SW Cypress Street. (There is a traffic light here; south of the highway this is called Minter Bridge Road.) Cypress curves to the right, becoming 32nd Avenue. Turn left onto Maple, left onto 31st Court. A narrow driveway entrance is immediately on the right.

Amenities:

Bridge at
Turner Creek.
*Photo by
Susan Peter*

10 ROOD BRIDGE ROAD PARK

This large new park at the junction of Rock Creek and the Tualatin River has a great deal to offer: mowed lawns, wild riparian woodlands, stately groves, a boat ramp, a small conference center, and ample parking. A 1.5-mile paved trail borders the river, goes around a large pond, and passes trickling waters.

Until 1991 the riverside portion of this property was privately owned. Thanks in large part to volunteer efforts, the wild area along the river is almost totally free of non-native plants. Mature bigleaf maples and Oregon ash shade a carpet of fringe-cups, yellow wood violets, and wild strawberries. Look for licorice fern growing on the maples, and sword fern proliferating between the Oregon-grape and snowberry. A few evergreens on the bank include red-cedar, grand fir, and Douglas-fir.

A pond provides good habitat for Hooded Mergansers, Canada Geese, and pond plants and other slimy things. On drier days, one can follow the path around the pond. If the path is flooded, stop and admire the reflections of the gray-green lichen-covered trees in the still waters, and the contrast between the wine-red stems of red-osier (creek) dogwood and the yellow bark of the adjacent willow thicket.

If the river level is not too high, a small footbridge across Rock Creek will be accessible. From there, a path leads downriver where less-developed trails pass through a coniferous woodland. A higher woodland, above the grassy lawns, is a typical Douglas-fir forest with vine maple and hazel in the understory and salal on the forest floor. Here, a Bewick's Wren hops through the understory. Its pretty song ends in a thin trill.

In addition to the paved paths, over a mile of soft trails invite exploration. Check them out to find duckfoot and foxgloves in the shaded woods, and self-heal and moth mullein in the sunshine.

Beaver live in the river, deer pass through the park; the many birdhouses set high in the trees encourage nesting birds. The remainder of the park has lovely landscaping that will delight your visitors or grandchildren. There are a pair of stone bridges, wide sloping lawns, tiny creeks with waterfalls, and old-fashioned street lights. This would be a good place to hold a family picnic.

Directions: From Tualatin Valley Highway (Hwy. 8) take River Road southeast to Rood Bridge Road. Turn right at the light, but do not drive into Hillsboro High School. Instead, follow the road around to the left for 0.2 miles. The park is on the left behind the fancy black metal fence.

Amenities:

VIEWING AREA 3: Beaverton Creek

Viewing Sites

1. Downtown Beaverton Creek Walk
2. Millikan Way Light Rail Station
3. Beaverton Creek Wetlands Park
4. Tualatin Hills Nature Park
5. Pheasant Park
6. Whispering Woods Park
7. Arleda Park
8. Sutherland Meadows Park

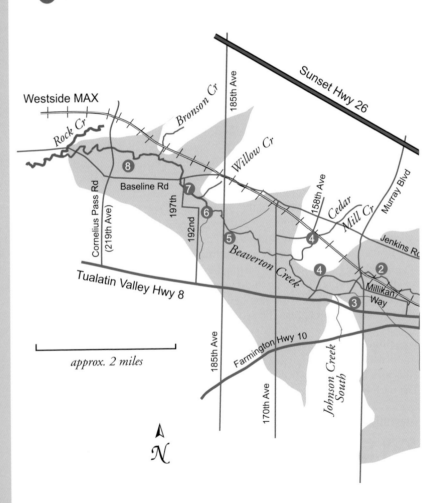

VIEWING AREA 3: Beaverton Creek

Beaverton Creek flows westward because most of its tributaries rise in the Tualatin Mountains (Portland's West Hills). Golf Creek's headwaters are seen pooled in the wetlands at the intersection of Miller and Barnes roads and flow under Highway 26 and Canyon Road near 96th Avenue before being met by Hall Creek in Kennedy Park. Hall Creek is first seen in a tiny rivulet flowing into a private pond near SW 87th and Birchwood Road. Additional branches, flowing in from the north and south along the Highway 217 corridor, once gathered the waters of Beaverton Creek into a fine marshy home for beavers right in downtown Beaverton. Now we see these channeled together and directed to the west, paralleling the light rail line until they bend south toward Beaverton Wetlands Park. Three more streams from the south join Beaverton Creek before Cedar Mill Creek adds its waters in Tualatin Hills Nature Park. Traveling northwest through a mostly protected natural corridor, Beaverton Creek flows into Rock Creek just west of the intersection of Baseline and Cornelius Pass roads.

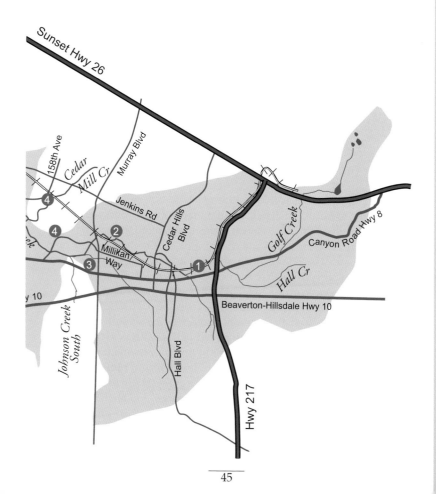

① DOWNTOWN BEAVERTON CREEK WALK

Mallard with ducklings.
Photo by Jim Cruce

While most of us think that natural beauty is found in rural settings, and much of the Tualatin Basin is still rural, it is a paradox that the easiest places to access the streamside and enjoy its quiet coolness and wildlife are often in town. This is well illustrated along Beaverton Creek, especially now that restoration work has reversed some earlier damage to the habitat. A walkable route of about a mile follows the creek through downtown Beaverton.

On 114th Avenue, just north of the MAX light rail tracks, a bridge provides a good view of ponds adjacent to the flowing creek where you can often see ducklings in the spring. When this area was torn up for light rail construction, great thickets of blackberries were removed and replaced with native plants. Now, standing in the creek among the sharp-edged, brown-blooming sedges, Great Blue Herons watch for darting fish. Dainty little blue *Veronica* flowers trail in the flowing water and Red-winged Blackbirds perch on small willows.

South of the tracks an asphalt walkway leads west, crossing the creek. In the summer, there are small patches of pungent, yellow-buttoned tansy. In a few more steps, a tiny bit of forest seems to surround the pathway. Overhead, there are Oregon ash and cherry; look for the characteristic twin "buds" at the base of each long, finely serrated leaf. Horsetail, sword fern, and trailing blackberry flourish in the dense undergrowth. Enormous six-foot-tall bracken fern grows here, too. Then, with each step west, Himalayan blackberry starts reinvading the creek. Step a few feet into the cool forest on one of the small dirt paths and notice the summer heat fall away at the water's edge. Before the paved path connects to SW 117th Avenue, look to the left across the creek to find an ornamental variety of English hawthorn. In May they are covered with bright pink blossoms.

Though the creek dives underground here at SW 117th, the path continues across the parking lot along grass, benches, and birch trees. Beaverton Creek can be found behind Learning Palace. There another tributary joins it, and a footbridge connects the path to the Beaverton Transit Center. From here to Cedar Hills Boulevard the creek is deeply trenched.

DOWNTOWN BEAVERTON CREEK WALK

This area, as well as the Fred Meyer/Beaverton Town Square, was all drained wetlands until the mid-1970s. The city was named "Beavertown" for a reason.

At the Transit Center, cross Lombard Avenue and, on the north side of the light rail line, follow Tri-Met's right of way; this is quite safe — the tracks are well fenced. Note the sequoia trees and native black hawthorns planted along this dirt path. Rejoin the creek after about a hundred feet and follow this path to Hall Boulevard.

The sidewalk on the west side of the Hall Boulevard Bridge provides an especially good view downstream because of the retention pond. Swallows dive overhead and Great Blue Herons and ducks are seen here every day. A raccoon family and several nutria live here.

Around the pond in this restored area, young black hawthorn trees have been planted as well as Oregon-grape, red-osier (creek) dogwood, oceanspray, the bright, magenta-flowered steeple bush, and the lovely wild rose. There are also abundant teasels. The teasel is a European import whose name comes from the early use of its prickly head to "tease" or raise the nap on woolen cloth. The creek continues westward behind a half-mile-long string of businesses but can again be viewed from the Center Street Bridge.

Tansy.
Photo by Susan Peter

Directions: From Highway 217, take the Hwy. 8 exit and head west (Tualatin Valley Highway/ Canyon Road). Almost immediately turn right onto 114th Avenue to the light rail crossing markers. Trail starts at the west end of McBride Court. If you arrive on MAX, start this walk at Beaverton Central Station or Beaverton Transit Center Station and walk all or part of this route in reverse.

Amenities:

Raccoons. *Photo by Jim Cruce*

2 MILLIKAN WAY LIGHT RAIL STATION

Here is excellent access to about a mile of Beaverton Creek parallel to the light rail line and Tektronix. The stream here is not deeply trenched and almost meanders by comparison to the previous stretch. Tall grasses and native shrubs would make for a perfect riparian zone if there were also some trees to shade the creek and keep it cool for native fish habitat. Nevertheless, the local Great Blue Heron fishes from here; you may see it perched on top of a storm water outflow pipe. Shrubs provide homes for Song Sparrows.

There are both sedges and rushes in the wetland. Both are grass-like in general appearance with clumps of two-foot-tall green "blades," and both have tufts of scratchy-looking brown flowers and seed heads. Touch them and take a closer look to find some of their differences. A cross section of sedge is solid and sharply triangular, but the rush stems are smooth tubes, usually filled with a soft white foamy pith. Hence the saying "sedges have edges and rushes are round; grasses have joints and come from the ground." Grasses have hollow stems, with jointed segments where the blades leave the stem. Bamboo is a grass; think of the joints in a bamboo pole. Rushes and sedges are generally without joints.

Two little roads cross the creek here, and near the western road are a pond and an island constructed for wildlife. Here you might find Hooded Mergansers: the males have a vertical fan-shaped white crest edged with black; the females' crests are tawny. Canada Geese rest on the little island. Farther west, the mudflats offer habitat for Long-billed Dowitchers, Spotted Sandpipers, and Western Sandpipers.

Directions: From Highway 217 go west on Tualatin Valley Highway (Hwy. 8) about a mile. Right on SW Hocken Avenue. Left on SW Millikan Way. Right on SW 141st Avenue. Beaverton Creek is north of the tracks.

Amenities:

Spotted Sandpiper.
*Photo by
Michael Wilhelm*

This natural-looking habitat consists of 15 acres at the confluence of Beaverton Creek and Johnson Creek South. As well as the usual waterfowl, look for Red-winged Blackbirds and three species of swallows: Barn Swallows show deeply forked tails and orange bellies, Violet-green Swallows sport white rump patches, and Bank Swallows have brown backs and a dark breast-band and a fluttery flight pattern.

Tall reed canarygrass is the dominant plant in this large area of reconstructed ponds and islands. It is a non-native, spreads rapidly through wetland areas, and out-competes native species. Though landscaped with native bushes and trees, much of the beginning of the trail is lined with Himalayan blackberries and it can be difficult to see the wetlands. Farther along this half-mile, all-weather path, the ground rises and there are two viewing areas, both with benches and one with a helpful interpretive sign. Shortly after, the asphalt ends and a dirt path turns away from the wetland and across private land.

Two of the plants shown on the interpretive sign are bulrushes. Bulrushes are the exception to the "sedges have edges" mnemonic mentioned on the previous page. Bulrushes, in spite of their name, are part of the Sedge Family, and while the stems of some species have the triangular cross section expected of a sedge (e.g., small-fruited bulrush), others are smoothly cylindrical, like rushes (e.g., softstem bulrush). Should you care to inspect them closely, you'll find that leaves of sedges have closed sheaths (the leaf bases are fused around the stem) but leaf sheaths of rushes are open at the base.

There are 50 species of sedges and rushes in the Pacific Northwest. Only six are identified specifically in this guide, and most of our references are general. Distinct shapes of flower heads may become apparent if you look for them; some are spherical clusters, some a spray of florets, some have several long thin spikes of inflorescence, often drooping. Rushes and sedges are frequently a part of stream restoration work for two important reasons: they provide nesting material, food, and shelter for many insects, birds, and small mammals, and they are valuable for removing heavy metals and excess nutrients from polluted water.

For an elevated (and quieter) view of this wetland, walk north on 153rd Avenue, which crosses Beaverton Creek here.

Directions: Paved trail begins at the northwest corner of Tualatin Valley Highway (Hwy. 8) and 153rd Avenue (a long block west of Murray Boulevard). There is no on-street parking nearby and all the parking lots are private. We recommend using MAX. The Beaverton Creek Light Rail Station is a very pleasant half mile away.

Amenities:

Swallows of the Tualatin

By Brian Wegener

San Juan Capistrano has nothing on the Tualatin River Basin. Every spring, like clockwork, six different species of swallows return to the Tualatin Basin to nest. The dramatic flight of swallows darting after flying insects is most entertaining. But their aerobatics aren't the only interesting thing about the swallows of the Tualatin — their nesting habits are fascinating, too.

Barn Swallow feeding fledgling.
Photo by Jim Cruce

Our Swallows Have a Variety of Interesting Nesting Habits

Northern Rough-winged Swallows, like Belted Kingfishers, excavate their nests in soft clay or sandy riverbanks. Look for holes four to five inches in diameter in recently eroded riverbanks. Depending on the hardness of the bank material, the depth of their burrows will range from one to five feet deep. Just a few feet away in the same bank you may see a Belted Kingfisher nest.

Two of our swallow species, the Tree Swallow and the Violet-green Swallow, typically nest in hollow trees. Violet-green Swallows are common to the cities and suburbs of the Portland metro area. If you would like to attract these mosquito-control agents to your backyard, they will use nesting boxes placed under the eaves of your house. To keep invasive House Sparrows from these nesting boxes, make an oval-shaped entrance hole in the box 7/8 inches high by three inches wide. Overall dimensions of the box should be five inches deep by eight inches wide by six inches high. Tree Swallows will also use nesting boxes. Tree Swallows have been known to use nesting boxes on bluebird trails. If Tree Swallows take over a bluebird nesting box, an additional box placed nearby will still be used by bluebirds.

The Barn Swallow and the Cliff Swallow build mud nests, reinforced by grass, feathers, or other found fiber. Before human settlement drastically changed the environment, most of these nests were built under rocky, naturally overhanging cliffs. Construction of homes, barns, bridges, and other structures that provide support and overhead shelter have increased the population of both of these species. You can tell the difference between Barn Swallow nests and Cliff Swallow nests by their shape and how they are attached to the structure they are built on. Barn Swallows prefer some type of support or shelf to build their cup-shaped nests on, such as a timber or bridge girder. In contrast, Cliff Swallow nests have been described as gourd-shaped. Unlike Barn Swallows, Cliff Swallows build a roof on their nests. Both need an overhang to keep the mud nest from dissolving in the rain.

The largest member of the Swallow Family, the Purple Martin, is rare in the Tualatin Basin. They have been seen nesting near the dam at Hagg Lake. In the eastern U. S. and the Midwest, Purple Martins are known for their colonial nesting habits. Traditionally farmers of the Midwest have erected "Martin Apartments" to attract the birds for insect control. On the West Coast,

Purple Martins do not use these apartments but nest in tree cavities excavated by woodpeckers or single nest boxes. Competition from European Starlings for nesting sites has reduced Purple Martin numbers.

Keys to Identifying the Swallows of the Tualatin

Swallows with similar nesting habits also have similar coloration. Both **Violet-green Swallows** and **Tree Swallows** have green backs and white undersides. The violet coloration at the base of the tail and the back of the neck on Violet-green Swallows is difficult to see except in ideal light. An easier way to tell the two apart is to look at the white patch on the cheek of the birds. On the Violet-green Swallow, the white patch extends above the eye, unlike the Tree Swallow which has dark green around the eye. Near the base of the tail, the white underside coloration extends almost all of the way across the back on the Violet-green Swallow.

The **Cliff Swallow** and the **Barn Swallow** have dark blue-black backs and buff to rust-colored undersides. The Cliff Swallow has a distinctive buff-colored patch on the rump and light patch above the beak. The most distinctive feature of the Barn Swallow is its deeply forked tail, which distinguishes it from all of our other species of swallow. The **Northern Rough-winged Swallow** has a light brown back and almost white underside. **Purple Martins** are larger than the other swallows and the males have a deep purple-blue coloration. Females are gray underneath.

Next time you are out on the river, look for our six species of swallows. Check the recently eroded banks for nests of the Belted Kingfisher and Rough-winged Swallows. When you paddle under a bridge, look up for the nests of Cliff Swallows and Barn Swallows, but beware of the pigeons.

Violet-green Swallow

Tree Swallow

Northern Rough-winged Swallow

Barn Swallow

Drawings by Barbara Macomber

4 TUALATIN HILLS NATURE PARK

The Tualatin Hills Nature Park is a natural gem set in the heart of Beaverton. Within its almost 200 acres, one can find most of the major habitats that occur in the Willamette Valley: oak-forested wetlands, ponds, meadows, creeks, and coniferous and deciduous forests. With this variety of habitats comes an assortment of animals ranging from coyotes to crawfish.

A good place to start is the Nature Park's Interpretive Center, which offers classes, a reference library, and a set of exhibits which discuss the region's ecology, habitats, and watershed. You will want to explore the over four miles of trails (1.5 miles of which is paved) that lead through groves of towering Oregon white oaks, along the banks of Cedar Mill and Beaverton creeks, through large groves of red-cedars and Douglas-firs and into open meadows. Several boardwalk areas provide excellent views of floodplains where beaver, mink, and deer tracks can regularly be seen. A glance skyward will likely afford a glimpse of any number of bird species including Pileated Woodpeckers, Winter Wrens, and a variety of warblers. The park also has several pond and wetland areas that, in the spring, attract throngs of breeding red-legged and Pacific chorus (tree) frogs. Throughout the year one can spot herons, kingfishers, and ducks along the waterways.

Any season is a great time to visit. Winter brings a variety of over-wintering birds and amphibian activities. Wildflowers abound in spring, while a verdant canopy is a cool summertime respite. Fall brings migratory birds, a brilliant show of changing leaf colors, and an assortment of mushrooms.

Directions: Take the MAX to the Merlo Road/158th Station. Cross tracks; face south. Turn left onto an asphalt path, "Oak Trail," which will lead you to the park's Interpretive Center (3/4 mile). From Tualatin Valley Highway (Hwy. 8) turn north on 160th at the traffic signal. (160th becomes Millikan Boulevard.) Driveway into park is on the left under the powerlines, less than a half mile from Tualatin Valley Highway.

Amenities:

The poisonous
Amanita mushroom.
Photo by Susan Peter

5 PHEASANT PARK

There are two useful access points into this undeveloped park.

Access 1: The paved trail runs about a hundred feet into a wooded glen. While the road noise from 185th is a bit distracting, a bench allows a pleasing view of the rippling summertime waters of Beaverton

Thimbleberry.
Photo by Susan Peter

Creek. The canopy of *big* bigleaf maples and red alders screened by red-cedars provides a cool home for a wide variety of plants and birds. You may see a Northern Flicker busy tapping out insects from a tree, while Douglas squirrels chatter from the branches.

Along the trail, fragrant fringe-cups, with their tall rigid stems of quarter-inch greenish-white blossoms, and buttercups add color April through June. Thimbleberry bushes (feel the very soft maple-shaped leaves — they are also known as "wood's toilet paper"), wild roses, vine maple, and Indian plum (oso berry) make up the understory of this typical native forest.

Access 2: Through this narrow access find natural trails that have been beaten into the creek's bottomlands.

Directions: Take Sunset Highway (Hwy. 26) or Tualatin Valley Highway (Hwy. 8) to 185th Avenue. SW Ewen is a side street 0.7 miles north of T. V. Hwy., two blocks north of the traffic light at Johnson Street.
Access 1: From SW 185th Avenue turn east on SW Ewen, then left on 184th Terrace. No off-street parking is provided. Follow the asphalt footpath down the hill between the houses at 18395 and 18415 SW Ewen.
Access 2: Continue east from 184th Terrace back onto SW Ewen. Find a narrow paved access between 18279 and 18287 SW Ewen.

Mink.
Photo by Jim Cruce

Whispering Woods Park is a protected little dell where the birds are often in full chorus. Remember to listen as you stroll through.

Blue elderberry. *Photo by Susan Peter*

Along the gravel entrance path, notice on the left the very large shiny leaves of a neighbor's magnolia tree. As this path enters the grassy clearing look, also on the left, for a blue elderberry bush with its large flat-topped flower clusters. The blooms smell a little like beer. Maple and Douglas-fir trees edge the lawn and shade a picnic table. Find ultra-lacy little filaree (closely related to wild geranium) along the edge of the trail. Filaree is also known as stork's bill because of the shape of its seedpod and is a non-native. Like those of the fringe-cups and common buttercups found in other parts of this park, filarees' basal leaves can be found in a thin carpet over the forest floor most of the year.

A paved loop dips down into the forest to a rivulet which it crosses on a pair of footbridges. Leave this paved path and follow unimproved side trails to reach Beaverton Creek. One of these trails leads to a second small stream; another goes through a thick stand of young red alder (look down for butter-cups) before entering a meadow. If it is February, you will quickly identify

Whispering Woods Park. *Photo by Brian Wegener*

the pussy willow tree there. Red-osier dogwood, snowberry, red alder, Himalayan blackberry, and the occasional large red-cedar form a thicket on Beaverton Creek's banks. On the hillside, as you return to the paved trail, notice that sword ferns, Oregon-grape, and salal are lush and green year-round under the cedar and Douglas-fir canopy. Licorice ferns cling to the older maple trees and are another wintertime treat for the eyes as you admire their leaflets zig-zagging across the center frond stem.

Laura Hill describes Whispering Woods as "a bird-watcher's dream." Birds of prey include Great Horned Owl and Red-tailed Hawk. Belted Kingfishers and Great Blue Herons both look for fish, but neither will turn down the occasional frog or salamander. Mallards and Wood Ducks swim among the patches of reeds. Bring your bird book to identify the various wrens. Also, there are Song Sparrows, Spotted Towhees, Black-capped Chickadees, Steller's Jays, and Bushtits.

Several small mammals enjoy this park; gray squirrels scold from trees, while the nocturnal raccoon is quite happy to forsake its natural diet to scavenge for the remains of someone's lunch. The deer mice prefer to eat small seeds.

Directions: Take Highway 26, Exit 64. South on 185th; turn right onto Baseline Road. Turn left (south) on SW 197th at the traffic light. Continue one-half mile and turn left on SW Stacey, right on SW 192nd. A Tualatin Hills Park and Recreation District sign marks the entrance.

Amenities:

Steller's Jay.

Western Scrub-Jay.
Photos by Jim Cruce

ARLEDA PARK

Access 1: An expansive short-grass meadow with some benches slopes down to Beaverton Creek. A half-mile paved loop trail goes to the water's edge, but access farther upstream to where Willow Creek joins the larger creek is blocked by seven-foot-tall reed canarygrass. In mid-summer the meadow fills with foot-high ox-eye daisy, false dandelion, red and white clovers, yellow bird's-foot trefoil, pale blue chicory, small morning glory (bindweed), Queen Anne's lace, purple self-heal, and pink centaury, all in a dusty-rose-colored foam of grass heads. Listen for grasshoppers, and watch for pretty yellow sulphur butterflies.

Access 2: The trail slopes down between backyards and under a small dense stand of red-cedar trees. In August, our botanist noted the bright pink, tubular flowers of hedge-nettle, and found fringe-cups, which bloom in May. The trail continues along to the right below fenced backyards for a couple of hundred yards before tall grass and brush eventually block the way. The trees here are mostly Oregon ash with some red alder. Our birdwatching observer was immediately greeted by a Downy Woodpecker and a Red-breasted Nuthatch working the trunk of an alder. Among the ashes and alders along the riparian zone he saw another Downy Woodpecker gleaning the small branches of a tree, with Cedar Waxwings feeding at the top of the tree. Black-capped Chickadees flitted about. On the ground, Song Sparrows and a Fox Sparrow were feeding. He heard the calls of American Robins and a Steller's Jay.

In a clearing maintained by one of the adjacent landowners, a female Western Tanager was feeding and a Western Wood-Pewee sallied from a dead branch. Cedar Waxwings flew back and forth between a tree and a birdbath, where they splashed noisily. White-crowned Sparrows could be seen in the blackberries, and a Mourning Dove cooed from the top of a snag. At the bottom of the snag, there was an oblong hole, a sign that a Pileated Woodpecker had been at work.

Directions: Hwy. 26, Exit 64. South on 185th; turn right onto Baseline.
Access 1: From Baseline Road turn south on 194th Avenue. Park is on right.
Access 2: From Baseline Road turn south on SW 197th (at the traffic light) and then left on Alderwood Court. A narrow grassy lane between house numbers 19595 and 19615 leads down to Beaverton Creek.

Amenities:

Downy Woodpecker.
Above photo by Michael Wilhelm

8 | SUTHERLAND MEADOWS PARK

This little park provides the last chance to explore Beaverton Creek before it flows into Rock Creek. There is an undefined grassy trail leading to a soggy meadow surrounding a couple of ponds. Step carefully or dress for mud. If you want to see the creek, look for it skirting around the north side of the ponds.

Mostly open meadowland, the park consists of tall and short grasses, small willows, and a thicket of Oregon ash. Waterfowl here include seasonally migrating geese. Listen for chickadees and jays in the tall Douglas-firs on the western side of the park. Neighbors say that raccoons, snakes, and a goodly number of amphibians all enjoy this 4.5-acre wetland.

Directions: Hwy. 26, Exit 64. South on 185th; turn right onto Baseline. From Baseline Road, turn north onto NW 211th Avenue, right onto NW Sutherland Way. Access is between 344 and 360 NW Sutherland Way.

Oregon ash
branch.
Notice the
teardrop-shaped
variation of the
end leaflet.

Oregon ash.
Photo by Susan Peter

AREA 3: Beaverton Creek

VIEWING AREA 4: Bronson, Willow, & Cedar Mill Creeks

Viewing Sites

1 Spyglass Park

2 Bronson Creek Park

3 Willow Creek Nature Park

4 Waterhouse Park

5 Salix Park

6 Cedar Mill Park

7 Jordan Park

8 Foothills Park

9 Commonwealth Lake Park

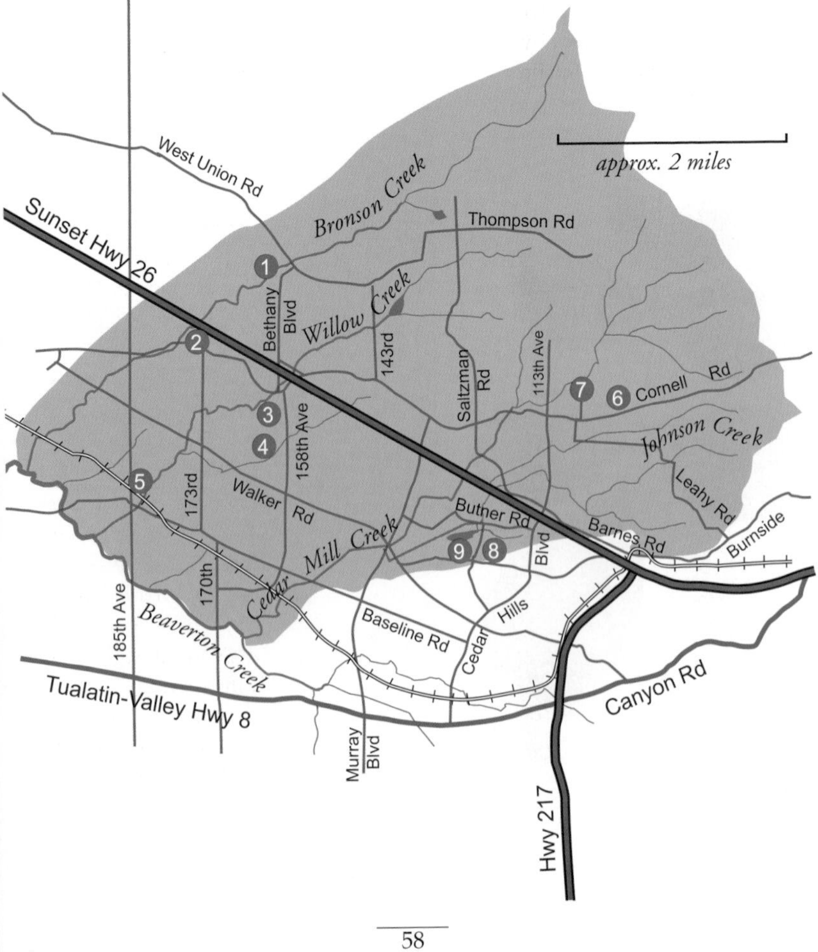

VIEWING AREA 4: Bronson, Willow, & Cedar Mill Creeks

These three creeks all rise in the Tualatin Mountains (West Hills) and flow to the southwest, reaching Beaverton Creek independently.

1. Bronson Creek, farthest west of the three, races down from Skyline crossing Laidlaw Road high up in the hills. Passing under Sunset Highway (Hwy. 26) near 173rd Street, it flows through a series of artificial lakes in the Tanasbourne area at 185th Avenue, south of Cornell Road. Farther south, beyond Walker Road, it passes near the rear corner of the Oregon Graduate Institute before flowing into Beaverton Creek just south of the MAX tracks and east of the Quatama station.

2. Willow Creek starts near Bonney Slope Park. After crossing under Sunset Highway, it enjoys protected corridors through the Waterhouse development and for much of its route to Beaverton Creek. Southwest of its crossing under the intersection of 185th Avenue and Baseline Road, it joins Beaverton Creek .

3. Cedar Mill Creek starts with several arms coming together at a small lake in the Forest Heights development along Miller Road north of Cornell. From here it flows southwest through Jordan Park. Just before crossing under Cornell Road it is joined by a tributary from Bonney Slope. (If you park east of 119th Avenue and the bridge, you can walk to a wooden sidewalk and peer deep into the dell below to see a lovely waterfall. This was once the site of a water-powered lumber mill.)

South of Cornell Road, Johnson Creek, a tributary of Cedar Mill Creek, collects runoff from the Leahy Road neighborhood. Below the Sunset Highway, Johnson Creek has been channeled and diverted to the benefit of Commonwealth Lake Park. It flows into Cedar Mill Creek at the intersection of Walker Road and Murray Boulevard. Cedar Mill Creek then becomes an integral part of the landscaping at Nike's World Headquarters. A boggy wetland is seen where Cedar Mill Creek crosses under Jenkins Road and the MAX Light Rail line just east of 158th Avenue. As it crosses under the tracks it enters the Tualatin Hills Nature Park where, deep in the forest, it joins Beaverton Creek.

Jordan Park (see page 67).
Photo by Susan Peter

1 SPYGLASS PARK

Western Pond Hawk. *Photo by Steve Berliner*

The 14 acres of Spyglass Park are predominantly a wetland meadow with a few small pockets of wetland forest and wetland scrub. Bronson Creek flows into Spyglass from the east and separates into two distinct channels that flow along the north and south edges of the park. A small dam creates a pond from a tributary that enters the park. The meadow is under water much of the year; the driest and therefore best time to visit Spyglass is in late spring or summer. The trails are primitive and seasonal. This park is wild and undeveloped.

The pond area provides excellent habitat for wetland mammals and birds. Red-winged Blackbirds, Hooded Mergansers, Mallards, Canada Geese, Violet-green, Tree and Barn swallows, Great Blue Herons, and Willow Flycatchers have been observed. Red-tailed Hawks nest in or near the park and can be seen soaring overhead. It was even reported that a very confused loon came to visit the pond during two winter seasons.

Other wildlife you might get a glimpse of at Spyglass Park includes beavers, muskrats, deer, coyotes, and raccoons. You can also find red-legged frogs and Pacific chorus frogs.

Although the park is heavily covered with invasive species such as reed canarygrass, bittersweet nightshade, and Himalayan blackberry, there are still opportunities to observe some beautiful native flora. Native vegetation includes tall alumroot, daggerleaf rush, tule, small-fruited bulrush, California figwort, blue-eyed-grass, and awl-fruited sedge. The wetland forest consists of Oregon ash, red-cedar, and red alder.

Directions: From Highway 26 take Exit 65. Follow signs to Bethany Boulevard. Travel north on Bethany Boulevard to West Union Road. Turn left on West Union. Left on Somerset Drive. Left on NW 164th Terrace. At the bottom of the hill, turn right on Joscelyn Street and park under the power lines. Or you can park on the south side of West Union Road, west of Bethany Boulevard, and attempt entry via the northeast corner of the park. The park is not signed.

Red-winged Blackbird on cat-tail.
Photo by Monte Rumgay

This simple little park is a great example of how a typical suburban patch of grass along a creek can be turned into a nature preserve friendly to both wildlife and neighborhood visitors.

If you come by in the spring, you will first notice the pale purple sheen of the meadow-foxtail grass with its soft, velvety panicles. Later, after producing pollen, the heads turn to orange. You will also notice the new plantings of maple, willow, and ninebark (so called because it was believed to have nine layers of bark on the stems). Ninebark's small leaves are maple-shaped and the white snowball flowers gradually develop heads of reddish seed husks; Native Americans used the wood for bows.

Mallards, Canada Geese, American Wigeons, and Common Mergansers visit the creek. An occasional Great Blue Heron joins the Belted Kingfisher to fish for sculpin and stickleback. There are also river otters, beaver, and even crawfish. By the creek, watch for big green dragonflies. These, long ago, were nicknamed "darners." Folklore has it that they would sew up the mouths of naughty children who told fibs.

Listen for the Red-winged Blackbird. In the spring his shoulder patches are brightly scarlet as he sings to stake out his territory. Song Sparrows and other backyard birds use the park, but the Barn Swallows with their rusty-orange undersides are a spectacular sight as they perform their nightly aerial ballet in search of insects. In the grass, busy mice and shrews nibble away at all kinds of seeds.

Directions: From Sunset Highway (Hwy. 26) take Exit 65. Following the signs for Hillsboro, go west on Cornell Road about 1.1 miles. The park is on the north side of the road just west of the light at 173rd Avenue.

Amenities:

Male Hooded Merganser.
Photo by Jim Cruce

WILLOW CREEK NATURE PARK

A boardwalk winds though this 13 acres of swampy bottomland of ash groves and willow thickets. Although threatened by non-native reed canarygrass and bittersweet nightshade, persistent natives can be found in the understory: red-osier dogwood, wild crabapple, Indian plum (oso berry), steeple bush, snowberry, clustered wild roses, and soft rush. The Friends of Rock, Bronson, and Willow Creeks are working to shade the creek, remove non-native plants, and replant with native trees, shrubs, sedges, and rushes. When mature, these native plants will shade the creek and provide food and shelter for fish and wildlife, including sculpins, beaver, kingfishers, towhees, and nuthatches.

Streamside willows and shrubs often are busy with Black-capped Chickadees, Bushtits, Bewick's Wrens, Song Sparrows, and Golden-crowned Sparrows. April and May are peak months for migrating songbirds. Look for Cedar Waxwings and Orange-crowned Warblers. Watch gangly Great Blue Herons stalk fish in shallow pools. The creek holds a persistent population of cutthroat trout. Scan the creek bottom for the orange shapes of crawfish. Rabbits scamper in the brush. You may find tracks of raccoons in the mud and on the boardwalk. Girdled trees indicate that the beavers are busy creating dams and marshy homes for themselves, muskrats, and other wildlife.

As you travel east into the Moshofsky Woods and Stonegate segments of the park, note that this is the largest block of forest habitat left on Willow Creek within the urban area. The bottomland is now bordered by a healthy Douglas-fir forest. A lush understory of vine maple, red elderberry, cascara, cherry, service berry, hazelnut, black hawthorn, mock orange, oceanspray, and baldhip rose is underlain by sword fern, salal, trailing blackberry, and Oregon-grape. There are pockets of western wahoo, an uncommon shrub that occurs primarily on Vancouver Island. Take time to dabble your toes beside the willows in the water. Look for secret places: hollow logs, mossy swales, and hidden animal niches.

Although birds can be seen year-round, activity peaks in spring. Walk the forest trails and search for warblers in wet swales and thickets. Trilliums and other wildflowers bloom from March through May. Look for rust-colored rough-skinned newts on the trails during and after rains from fall through spring. Do you see and hear the Douglas squirrels chattering in the trees? Listen for the haunting hoots of Great Horned Owls and the yip-yips of playful coyotes at dusk.

Rough-skinned newt.
Photo by Brian Wegener

Service berry. *Photo by Susan Peter*

AREA 4: Bronson, Willow, & Cedar Mill Creeks

The Winthrop Bike Path is a public passage through a privately owned part of the Willow Creek bottomlands and connects to the boardwalk, creating a 3/4-mile hard surface path the length of Willow Creek Nature Park, from 158th Avenue to 173rd. This path also connects to Waterhouse Park, one-half mile south of here, via the asphalt trails of the power-line parks.

At the west end of Willow Creek Nature Park, notice that the creek was straightened many years ago to expedite the passage of floodwaters. It is now attempting to reclaim a more natural winding passage through the floodplain. This **west entrance**, at 173rd Avenue, is across the street from Apollo Ridge Park. There are no trails into this sensitive wetland, but a walk through the church parking lot that borders Apollo Ridge Park may provide some views into the natural area.

Directions: From Highway 26 take Exit 65 to south side of freeway. Follow Walker Road Recreation Center signs to find NW 158th Avenue. This is a rather complex interchange. Go south on 158th a scant 0.1 mile before turning right on NW Waterhouse Avenue. Park entrance on the right. For access directly to Moshofsky Woods and Waterhouse segments: Continue west on NW Waterhouse Avenue. Turn right on Silverado Drive; right on Mission Oaks Drive; right on NW Winged Foot Terrace to park entrance.

West entrance: From Highway 26 take Exit 65. Following signs to Hillsboro, travel west one mile on Cornell Road. Turn left on NW 173rd Avenue and go approximately one-half mile to the creek. Tualatin Hills Park and Recreation District signs are on left and right. Park on a side street nearby.

Amenities:

Striped Meadowhawk (skimmer or dragonfly).

Vivid dancer (damselfly).

12-spotted skimmer.
Photos by Steve Berliner

4 WATERHOUSE PARK

A narrow band of ash, willow, red-osier dogwood, and native (black) hawthorn borders a small tributary of Willow Creek in this park. Streamside willows and shrubs chatter with sparrows, wrens, and blackbirds. Near the picnic tables and children's play equipment, a remnant grove of stately Oregon white oaks harbors an understory of cherry, Indian plum (oso berry), and snowberry. Downstream of the oak grove, a private pond provides home for waterfowl and aquatic mammals. This good, 1/4-mile paved trail continues west and then north to connect to Willow Creek Nature Park via Waterhouse Powerline Park. Its lovely old-style lampposts with tinted glass provide soft light which helps make this little park inviting for evening strolls to see and hear nocturnal creatures.

Look for gray squirrels in the oak grove and evidence of beaver and nutria along the creek and in the pond. Fish in the pond attract playful river otters. Watch Mallards (the males have curly tails), Buffleheads, and American Wigeons. Look for Willow Flycatchers, Wilson's Warblers, Yellow Warblers, and Common Yellowthroats in the spring. Red-winged Blackbirds, Spotted Towhees, Song Sparrows, and Golden-crowned Sparrows nest along the creek.

Great Horned Owl.
Photo by Michael Wilhelm

Directions: Highway 26, Exit 65 to south side of freeway. Follow Walker Road Recreation Center signs to find NW 158th Avenue. Go south on 158th 0.4 miles and turn right on NW Blueridge Avenue. Take Foxborough Circle south to the park entrance.

Amenities:

Yellow Warbler.
Photo by Steve Berliner

Salix Park is named for its willows; *Salix* is the botanical name for the willow, derived from the Celtic *sal* (near) and *lis* (water). Willow Creek gently meanders through this 3.9-acre natural area park where downed trees provide abundant cover for fish and aquatic insects. The steep east side of the creek is buffered by a mature Douglas-fir and red-cedar forest with several large Pacific yews. Red elderberry, service berry, oceanspray, Indian plum, sword fern, and salal add variety to the understory. The west side of the creek is wide and flat, dominated by ash, willow, and reed canarygrass, but with pockets of small-fruited bulrush, soft rush, *Veronica*, buttercup, and steeple bush. The terraces on the west side of the floodplain are cloaked in a narrow band of Douglas-fir, Oregon ash, red alder, Pacific willow, cascara, black hawthorn, snowberry, and wild rose. In winter the natural trails will be muddy, or even under water.

April and May are peak months for migrating song-birds. Over 70 species of birds have been seen in the park, including Red-tailed Hawk, Great Horned Owl, Great Blue Heron, Green Heron, Wood Duck, Red-winged Blackbird, Belted Kingfisher, Red-breasted Nuthatch, Varied Thrush, Spotted Towhee, Steller's and Western Scrub-Jays,

Varied Thrush. *Photo by Jim Cruce*

White-throated and Golden-crowned sparrows, MacGillivray's Warbler, and Wilson's Warbler. Look for bats and Vaux's Swifts harvesting mosquitoes from the late summer sky. The creek holds small fish such as sculpins and shiners. Look for mussel shells along the creek edge and snails attached to the side of the creek bank. Delicate water starwort clings to the shallows and peppery water-cress grows along the seeps. In summer look for courting dragonflies and damselflies near marshy vegetation. Nutria holes line the sides of the creek bank. To locate the beaver dam, listen for the sound of falling water. Sit quietly and you may hear the sound of voles and deer mice scurrying through the grass.

Directions: Take Highway 26, Exit 64. On NW 185th Avenue travel south 1.7 miles. Left onto Salix Terrace, follow to end. Turn right onto SW Salix Ridge. A Tualatin Hills Park and Recreation District sign marks some steps down to natural trails. Or, take Westside MAX light rail to 185th Avenue station and cross 185th at the light. There are two additional (unsigned) accesses at ends of cul-de-sacs in this little neighborhood.

Amenities:

6 CEDAR MILL PARK

AREA 4: Bronson, Willow, & Cedar Mill Creeks

Black-capped Chickadee. *Photo by Jim Cruce*

A large mowed lawn covers most of this five-acre park, although a small woodland full of bird song and chatter borders its west side and a tall old snag provides woodpecker habitat. Go just beyond the tennis courts and the grove of large Douglas-firs to where a lush green lawn is soggy with several seeps and springs. This is the headwaters of one of the many tributaries of Cedar Mill Creek.

Picnic tables and barbecue grills under the Douglas-firs invite a longer stay to enjoy the other large trees here. There are several exotics planted in a line along the parking lot following a pair of Douglas-firs: a sequoia, a noble fir, a small prickly Colorado blue spruce, and four or five white fir.

Along with the occasional Mallard, you will see all the usual backyard birds in Cedar Mill Park, but do keep your ears and eyes open for more unusual species. The Killdeer is a pretty, showy plover that echoes its name — a repeated "kill-deeah" signifies its presence. The Black-capped Chickadee also calls its own name; it has a very loud voice for such a little bird.

You may also notice two tree-climbing birds here: the little Brown Creeper, smaller than a sparrow, ascends each tree spirally before flying to the base of the next tree, while the Downy Woodpecker, slightly larger than a sparrow, has powerful feet and a stiff, spiny tail to act as props while climbing up trees looking for wood-boring insects.

Directions: From Highway 26 take Exit 68. Follow Cedar Hills Boulevard northbound for 0.8 miles. Turn right on NW Cornell Road. On the left, just beyond 107th Avenue, look for a Tualatin Hills Park and Recreation District sign facing Cornell Road. Cedar Mill Elementary School shares the parking lot.

Amenities:

7 JORDAN PARK

Follow a narrow path down into a steep-walled ravine that is thickly wooded with western red-cedar, red alder, and grand fir. It isn't just good fortune that this area appears to be one of the least disturbed areas in this guide. The Cedar Mill Creek Watershed Watch has worked hard to remove the Himalayan blackberry that chokes out native plants and destroys wildlife habitat. Their reward has been to enjoy the flying squirrels who make their homes here, as well as to observe a healthy bird population including American Kestrels and Peregrine Falcons.

Native red huckleberry bushes can be seen from the trail and salmonberry bushes try to grow across it. At one point the trail pushes around a large spreading wood fern. Note the subtle differences between it and the lady ferns that abound here. The lateral leaves on the lady fern's fronds are longest and widest at the middle of the stem, but decrease in size as they near the base of the plant. The lateral leaves of the spreading wood fern create a triangular frond, widest at the bottom. You can also find licorice fern here. See page 146.

A clear stream, Cedar Mill Creek, gurgles between large rounded boulders and over a rocky bottom of shale-like tilting bands of bedrock. The oxalis, or wood sorrel, is plentiful along the damp banks. A veritable garden of woodland wildflowers blooms beside a mile of natural paths that lace this 14.5-acre park. Look for liverwort among the mosses on the rocks and logs. "Wort" is the old English word for plant (i.e., liverplant or St. John's plant). In the fall you can find shelf fungi, mushrooms, and lichens, and of course, a variety of berries. Be sure to note the several different species of mosses here. Perhaps you will find a feather moss — a tiny green "feather" about 1.5 inches long.

Alternate access: A trail through a bog and grassland leads past a fine patch of skunk cabbage to the north side of the creek.

<u>Directions:</u> From Highway 26 take Exit 68. Follow Cedar Hills Boulevard northbound for 0.8 miles. Turn right on NW Cornell Rd. Turn left on 107th Avenue. Tualatin Hills Park and Recreation District sign marks the trailhead at the end of the road.
<u>Alternate access:</u> From NW Cornell Road, north on 113th Avenue. Right on Lost Park Drive. A vacant lot at the foot of Andrews Place has some steep stairs to the trailhead. No sign.

Oxalis (wood sorrel). *Photo by Susan Peter*

<u>Amenities:</u>

AREA 4: Bronson, Willow, & Cedar Mill Creeks

8 FOOTHILLS PARK

Appearances can be deceiving. Foothills Park appears to be quite small, but a second look shows that it is much more than just a mowed lawn with children's play equipment. A high trail north of the creek leads to basketball courts. Across the clear creek, take the low trail which leads to the woods. Look for evidence of moles here. They leave small volcanoes of dirt, but without visible holes. Obviously unwelcome in any well-tended garden, moles and gophers provide a valuable service in wild places as they aerate and mix the soil. Moles sniff out earthworms to eat; gophers are vegetarians, dining on roots and bulbs. Gophers leave an asymmetrical mound with an exposed hole. Along the edge of the path, notice the hedge-nettle, a member of the Mint Family. Crush a leaf. Unlike most other mints, this one stinks.

The chickadees like the open field here; they can retreat to the brush along the creek. Western Scrub-Jays are in constant conversation, warning each other of intruders. As the ravine narrows, a thick stand of red-osier (creek) dogwoods on the right provides food and shelter for more birds. The dogwoods also help slow winter's floodwaters to the benefit of a patch of skunk cabbages that, in the autumn, are many feet away from the stream. There are delicate lady ferns here too, which, like skunk cabbage, die back to the ground each winter.

Notice, too, the horsetails, one of the most widespread plants in the world and the first vascular plant to send up green shoots after the 1980 eruption of Mount St. Helens. Our most common horsetails have two forms: growing from underground rhizomes, they send up segmented straight stems (pink, if common horsetail or brown, if giant) in the early spring. Later, green stems covered with whorls of long coarse green hairs grow from these rhizomes. Touch them to feel their high silica content, which makes them useful for scouring. Both common and giant horsetail have these two forms. Other horsetails have only one form, some of them with only the bare stem, some with only token whorls, but all are recognizably related and found in wet places.

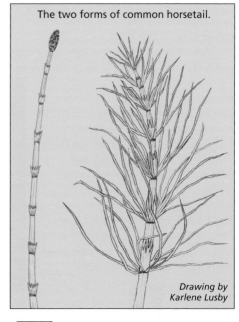

The two forms of common horsetail.

*Drawing by
Karlene Lusby*

Bewick's Wren.
Photo by Jim Cruce

As the trail leaves the stream and climbs into the woods of tall Douglas-firs, the underbrush thickens with red huckleberries, baldhip roses, large avens, ferns, and trailing blackberries. A "chip-chip" sound is heard in short bursts and the bushes rustle slightly. A small brown bird with a turned-up tail is jumping from twig to twig underneath the dense cover. Feeding on this abundance of berries? No, this is a Bewick's Wren feeding on insects who are themselves enjoying the berries, no doubt.

Low on the ground, find feather moss growing amid the many other mosses, slimy liverworts, and dry-looking lichens; they all like the cool, damp environment.

English ivy, small English hawthorn, and English holly are all non-natives whose presence is a problem. There are many other small wildflowers here that would truly thrive if it were not for these aggressive foreigners. Even large trees suffer from the strangling ivy vines. Hawthorns and hollies re-seed prolifically, forcing out hazels, elderberries, vine maples, and other small trees. Call your local parks department to join the "No-Ivy Leaguers." Visit their website, www.noivyleague.com.

Note that across the street from the 10 acres of Foothills Park lie the very different 23 acres of Commonwealth Park.

Directions: Highway 26 to Exit 68. Immediately south of the freeway turn right onto Butner Road. Follow Butner Road 0.5 miles. Turn left on SW Huntington. While the showier Commonwealth Lake Park is on the right, Foothills Park is on the left. No off-street parking.

Amenities:

9 COMMONWEALTH LAKE PARK

This delightful lake was created in 1965 by a developer who deepened a natural wetland and trenched the main channel of Johnson Creek, which forms the park's northern boundary. Foothills Creek and a portion of Johnson Creek flow into the east end of the lake. Natural springs under the lake add to these waters. In very cold winters, when most of the lake freezes over and it becomes a neighborhood ice-skating pond, these slightly warmer underground sources are evident.

The diversion from Johnson Creek comes into a small, round pool before it flows under a footbridge. This is a favorite spot for ducklings, and has a nice variety of aquatic plants. Indian rhubarb and red-stemmed prostrate spurge grow on the soggy bank. The straightened main channel of Johnson's Creek is edged with steeple bush, teasel, and several varieties of rush.

A 0.8-mile paved path circles the lake and several viewing platforms and bridges are especially welcome, as are the excellent descriptive sign boards.

Rosa rugosa, with its large, simple blooms, large round hips, and forbidding thorns, is very effective in keeping trespassers out of nesting areas. Look for the tall beggar-tick. It is a rayless composite with a tiny flower on a five-foot tall stalk and is planted for wildlife habitat. Beggars and other travelers brushing against this plant would find their clothes covered with its microscopically barbed seeds.

Fishing, with a license of course, is popular here; the lake is stocked with bass and rainbow and cutthroat trout. There are also bluegills, crappies, catfish, suckers, and squawfish. A 1996 inventory by Brad Stark (a seventh-grader at the time) lists muskrats and beavers in the lake as well as turtles and crawfish. There are all the usual backyard birds, including Common Ravens and flocks of Brewer's Blackbirds. In the summer listen for the "wichety-wichety" call of the Common Yellowthroat.

Great Blue Herons, Wood Ducks, and Cormorants can sometimes be seen here. And in the fall there are great numbers of American and Eurasian wigeons. Note the difference between these ducks. Both have white pinstripes on their black tails, but the male American Wigeon has a white crown and green band on his head; the male Eurasian Wigeon has a buff-colored crown on a rufous, or rosy-colored, head. You may expect to see Buffleheads, too, and always swimming with the ducks are black American Coots with their distinctive white beaks.

Mallards are everywhere on the lake. They feed by upending and dabbling, and though they can dive, they seldom do. When frightened they spring into the air instead of taxiing along the water. The large "herd" of geese asserts itself along the pathway. These aggressive birds, beaks high and emitting groaning honks, surely inspired the term "goose stepping!" Obviously, people have been giving handouts to these geese.

So, a caution is in order. If you must feed the waterfowl, bring dry corn kernels, not bread, which harms the birds and pollutes the lake. Sprinkle the corn from a bridge or viewing spot to keep your small children well away from the geese.

Directions: Highway 26 to Exit 68. Immediately south of the freeway, turn right onto Butner Road. Follow Butner 0.5 miles. Left on SW Huntington. Commonwealth Lake Park is on the right.
Alternate Access: Continue on Huntington one block to Foothills Drive. Turn right to reach a well-marked entrance at Dellwood Avenue. No off-street parking at either location.

Amenities:

Eurasian Wigeon.
Photo by Steve Berliner

American Wigeon
(baldpate).
Photo by Monte Rumgay

Little Flowers
Photos by Susan Peter

Cornflower

Centaury (Rosita)

Vetch

Large avens

Filaree (stork's bill)

English (black) plantain

Broad-leaved plantain

Haines Falls, above Cherry Grove. *Photo by Michael Wilhelm*

The Tualatin River Paddling Trail

Paddling from Cherry Grove to Fern Hill Road
By Paul Whitney

• **Cherry Grove,** South Road Bridge: River Mile 67.83
This is the farthest upriver access point to the Tualatin River. Above Cherry Grove, the Tualatin is truly a cascading mountain stream with frequent rapids and waterfalls. Salmon redds (nests in the gravel created by the female with her tail) have been observed in this area, and local residents catch steelhead near the bridge. Above the bridge, the river is closed to the public, but access is available during some of the Tualatin Riverkeepers' van tours or other special events along the upper river. For an overview of this stretch of the river, see the map on page 2.

Please note that while winter flows are adequate for canoeing, only the expert should attempt the river during this season. Summer flows below South Bridge are shallow for canoeing, and some dragging is generally needed; the riverbed is angular basalt rocks and boulders that would damage canvas or kevlar canoes. Because the difficulties of portaging the many logjams between here and Gaston, and the need to pre-arrange permission to cross private property, most canoeists would rather not attempt this portion of the river. This account, by an expert paddler, relates his observations and experiences.

Downstream the character of the river changes dramatically and the substrate becomes a rounded, river-washed cobble. The closed canopy of mixed coniferous-deciduous forest found upstream becomes a narrow band of deciduous trees and shrubs. About halfway between South Road Bridge and the Mt. Richmond Road Bridge there are no trees at all. Along the cut bank in this area erosion is extreme and tons of sediment are delivered to the river every year. The erosion is most likely due to plowing too close to the river and to the absence of bank-stabilizing vegetation.

Just before Mt. Richmond Road the logjams are nasty and require short portages along farm access roads. This is private property and must be respected accordingly. Cutthroat trout fishing above and below Mt. Richmond Road is good. All along the river there are signs of bank fishing: empty bait cans, bobbers, and monofilament line.

• **Mt. Richmond Road Bridge**: River Mile 65.9
Summer canoeing immediately below Mt. Richmond Road Bridge is pleasant but requires maneuvering around and over small logjams. Hazards in this area include protruding sections of metal pipe and miscellaneous junk. Cut banks in this reach reveal protruding organic debris, the remnants of active flooding and channel movement.

There are many logjams between Mt. Richmond Road and Gaston. These logjams are comprised of large woody debris that is anchored to the bank and provides ideal cutthroat trout habitat. Trout are easily caught in this reach when water temperatures are cool. Warm and low water in July, 2001, produced no trout in this otherwise productive reach. These logjams are also important to a variety of wildlife for cover and foraging.

All but one of these logjams are negotiable or easily portaged around. An extended floating logjam above Gaston is particularly difficult to negotiate because it covers 100% of the river for about a half mile. Since the logs and debris are floating, one cannot walk on the logs without sinking. This jam is a hazard for boaters and should be avoided. The banks are very steep (near vertical) on both sides and a portage around necessitates climbing about 15 feet up and out of the river channel. The land up top is private and one must arrange in advance for permission to portage or take out.

This area of the floating jam is the first extended reach of flat water as the Tualatin comes out of the Coast Range. This logjam is unique in that it covers all of the river and appears to preclude sunlight penetration into the water.

Above Gaston the riparian forest widens, and birds of prey such as the Goshawk and Cooper's Hawk are likely to be seen. They hedge-hop among trees and thickets, flying with several short, quick beats and a glide as they hunt birds and small mammals. There are plenty of signs of deer here, and trees gnawed by beavers are everywhere. Cougar, coyote, and black bear have been seen nearby.

• **Gaston**, Old State Highway 47: River Mile 64.25
This much less traveled road is just a stone's throw to the west of new Highway 47, but access is possible under both highway bridges.

The reach below Gaston is one of the more difficult due to logjams and the need to portage. This area of the river underwent major reconstruction when Wapato Lake was separated from the Tualatin. Structures related to filling and emptying the lake are noticeable. Above the river's confluence with Scoggins Creek the current is swift, but below, where the flow doubles, the substrate changes to mud and fine sediment. The water from Scoggins Creek is noticeably cooler than the Tualatin water. This is probably due to water releases from the bottom of Hagg Lake.

Access points (and hazards) from Rood Bridge to Shipley Bridge

The Tualatin Riverkeepers publishes *Paddler's Access Guide to the Lower Tualatin River*. For a copy, contact them at 503-590-5813 or info@tualatinriverkeepers.org

- **Rood Bridge Road Park**, Hillsboro: River Mile 38.4 LB*
See page 43. Turn right as you enter to get to the boat ramp.

- **Eagle Landing,** Scholls: River Mile 29.6 LB
From Highway 210, turn left onto Rainbow Lane at Groner School. Travel 1.3 miles to the far corner of this loop road to a small parking lot and short gravel path to river.

- **Scholls Bridge,** Scholls (undeveloped): River Mile 26.9 LB
On Highway 210 (Scholls Ferry Road) north of Scholls-Sherwood Road. Informal access on northeast end of the bridge. The trail to the river is steep and slippery.

- **Schamburg Bridge**, Sherwood (undeveloped): River Mile 16.2 RB
Take Highway 99W to Beef Bend Road. Turn left onto Roy Rogers Road. Bridge is on Roy Rogers Road just north of Scholls-Sherwood Road. Park on the shoulder. BEWARE OF TRAFFIC! Access the river on the southwest end of the bridge on county road right-of-way. The path to the river is steep and slippery.

- **Highway 99W Bridge** at Hazelbrook Road, Tualatin: River Mile 11.5 RB
(wheelchair accessible) *Take Highway 99W and turn south on SW 124th. Turn east onto Tualatin Road. Turn north on SW 115th Avenue. Turn left onto Hazelbrook Road.*

- **Cook Park**, Tigard: River Mile 9.8 LB
See page 132. Bypass the picnic grounds and keep going south until you come to the boat ramp and dock.

> **CAUTION: Rocks**: River Mile 9.3
> Just upstream from Fanno Creek and the railroad bridge the river becomes very shallow during summer. If the diversion dam is down, beware of rocks.

- **Tualatin Community Park**, Tualatin: River Mile 8.9 RB
See page 133. Stay on south side of railroad trestle and turn right to get to boat ramp.

- **Brown's Ferry Park**, Tualatin: River Mile 7.5 RB
See page 140.

- **Rivergrove Boat Ramp**, Rivergrove: River Mile 7.4 LB
(Picnic facilities, wheelchair accessible) *From I-5 take Exit 290. Take Lower Boones Ferry Road towards Lake Oswego. Turn right onto Pilkington. Turn right onto SW Childs Road. Within two blocks, turn south onto SW Marlin Court. Turn right onto Dogwood Drive and park. Small boat ramp is located between two houses on the south side of Dogwood Drive. Rivergrove Park is across the street from the ramp and offers a mowed lawn, 1950's style playground equipment, and ample street parking.*

- **Stafford Road-Shipley Bridge** (undeveloped): River Mile 5.4 LB
From I-205 take Exit 3. Follow Stafford Road across Borland Road. Cross Shipley Bridge, turn right immediately onto Shadow Wood Drive and follow it down to the water. There is gravel shoulder parking for about two cars.

> **HAZARD: Lake Oswego Corporation Diversion Dam**: River Mile 3.45
> There is a low head dam two miles downstream from Shipley Bridge (Stafford Road). It is impassable and dangerous. There is a warning sign, but there is no portage around it. STAY AWAY!

*LB = left bank, presuming you are facing downstream. RB = right bank.

West Linn Area: Two little paddling trips on the Tualatin River Trail

• **Fields Bridge**, West Linn (undeveloped): River Mile 1.7 LB*
Take I-205 Exit 3. Follow Stafford Road north to Borland Road and turn right. Highway 212 (Borland Road - Willamette Falls Drive) uses Fields Bridge to cross the Tualatin at the west edge of West Linn. Barely 20 feet from the east end of the bridge, turn north on Dollar Street. You'll find parking for a few cars. The access point is under the bridge.

Rocks will keep you from going too far downstream, but you can paddle upstream for about a mile before rocks and rapids will stop your progress. Tualatin River Wetlands Park (River Mile 2.4) is about 3/4 of a mile upstream. In the winter months with flows of 1500CFS, experienced white-water canoeists and kayakers enjoy the rapids downstream of Fields Bridge.

• **Willamette Park**, West Linn: River Mile 0.0 LB
See page 150. This site provides paddling access to the Willamette and the last few hundred yards of the Tualatin. Shallow rocky rapids immediately upstream will keep you from getting very far on the Tualatin.

A Few Words on Paddling Safety

Any time you are on the river, play it safe by following a few safety rules:
- Always wear a Coast Guard-approved personal flotation device.
- Don't drink and paddle. Alcohol or drugs can impair your ability to respond to dangerous situations.
- Don't paddle alone. Let someone know your plans.
- Carry a whistle or other signal device.
- Don't paddle during hazardous conditions.
- Be aware of the weather, currents, river conditions, and time of day.
- Wear appropriate clothing, including footwear and hat. Avoid sunburn and hypothermia. Take extra clothing in a waterproof container.
- Take food and water. Paddling is hard work.
- Avoid downed trees, dams, irrigation pumps, and other hazards in the river.

Winter Safety
Winter canoeing is not to be taken lightly. Due to the large number of overhanging trees, downed trees and logjams in the river, winter currents can make it a dangerous place to paddle. Don't put yourself into a deadly situation. Make sure you know the situation on the river and don't overestimate your paddling skills.

If you fall in the water you have about 15 minutes to get out and get warmed up. EXPOSURE is a DEADLY HAZARD. Always take a change of dry clothes in a waterproof duffel. Tie the duffel into the canoe.

---

*LB = left bank, presuming you are facing downstream. RB = right bank.

VIEWING AREA 5: Beaverton's Johnson Creek

Beaverton's Johnson Creek flows from the north slopes of Cooper and Sexton mountains. The longest tributary rises on Cooper Mountain near SW 185th and Gassner Road, and is joined by a more central branch in Summercrest Park. Farther east, Sexton Mountain tributaries flow through Beacon Hill and Sexton Mountain parks before joining the main stream at the foot of Vale Park. Smaller branches join Johnson Creek at Lowami Hart Woods and Brookhaven parks. The creek then flows through the wide green bottomland seen between Farmington and Tualatin Valley highways. It joins Beaverton Creek in the wetlands park just north of Tualatin Valley Highway.

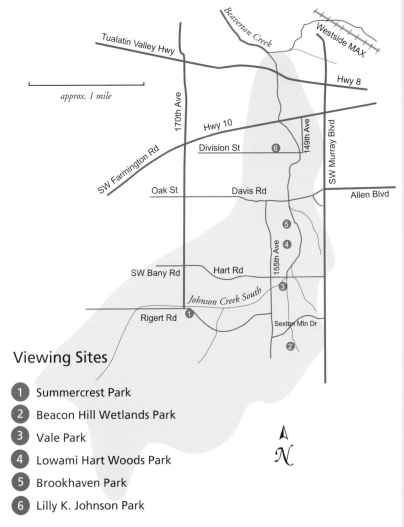

Viewing Sites

1. Summercrest Park
2. Beacon Hill Wetlands Park
3. Vale Park
4. Lowami Hart Woods Park
5. Brookhaven Park
6. Lilly K. Johnson Park

1 SUMMERCREST PARK

AREA 5: Beaverton's Johnson Creek

On the north side of Johnson Creek, mowed grass gives access to a fine little wetland. Although it is too wet for trees, tall cat-tails and a six-foot-tall species of rush provide some shade for the water. On higher ground, but still with wet feet, is a small stand of Oregon ash and native willows, and a large old weeping willow (an import originally from China). Higher up the bank, steeple bush, native trailing blackberries, oaks, and wild roses like their soil slightly drier.

Marsh Wren. *Photo by Jim Cruce*

South of the stream, a half-mile paved path connects with trails in Burntwood and Hart Meadows Powerline parks. Here at the west end of Summercrest, note a large, old black hawthorn (native) growing amidst the wall of Himalayan blackberries (non-native, but good picking in August). If you are lucky here, you may spot a Marsh Wren. Follow the path east for shaded picnic tables, elevated barbecues, and a children's play area.

Cross 165th. Listen to the birds; you may hear the "coo-coo-coo" of the Mourning Dove. Keep still and watch. Song Sparrows are quite common; they have heavily streaked breasts and pump their tails when they fly. There are Yellow Warblers here, too, but it's hard to distinguish between the many varieties of these brightly-colored little songbirds.

In a small meadow, note the beaver-chewed trees. Slightly farther east, it is easy to find a dirt trail into a stand of mature oaks and Douglas-firs. English ivy has invaded the forest floor. Watch out for occasional poison oak in the understory of large hazel bushes and young Oregon ash.

Almost to the power lines that parallel SW 160th Avenue, a clearing created by playing children gives more light to the forest floor, and native trailing blackberry becomes the carpeting vegetation while low snowberry, service berry, English holly, and Oregon-grape form the understory.

<u>Directions</u>: From Farmington Road turn south on SW 170th Avenue. Travel 1.5 miles to SW Rigert Road; turn left and park.

<u>Amenities:</u>

2 BEACON HILL WETLANDS PARK

This steeply sloping watercourse is the southern arm of Johnson Creek. It has been converted to a series of ponds terraced by small earthen dams and tucked between backyards. A faint trail follows the stream only a short distance. In August the waters of these upper ponds are virtually covered with an amazing assortment of native and introduced aquatic plants. Some, such as the non-native fragrant water-lily, red-stemmed prostrate spurge, and clover-fern, are rooted in the mud below the waters. Others, such as duckweed and the lacy red-leafed water-fern, are merely minute floating leaves, each tiny cluster having a few dangling roots. Don't expect these two ferns to look very fern-like. The water-fern at least has divided leaves, but "clover" is the descriptive part of the common name "clover-fern."

Hundreds of non-native bullfrogs enjoy these waters, as do Mallards, and even an occasional Green Heron. Around the pond are weeping willows and corkscrew willows (Chinese imports), and the tall, ever-beautiful, ever-invasive, purple loosestrife.

View the largest pond from the park's lower end on SW Turquoise Loop at SW 154th Avenue where water birds can be enjoyed from a distance. There is no access into the park from this end.

Directions: From Highway 217 follow Scholls Ferry Road west to Murray Boulevard. Right on Murray. Left on Beard Road. Right on 155th; right on Emerald Street. Follow Emerald Street up the hill and see Tualatin Hills Park and Recreation District sign on left.

Delicate duckweed floats
on the pond's surface.
Photo by Susan Peter

Bullfrogs are commonly
seen pond residents.
Photo by Jim Cruce

3 VALE PARK

Here, the western branch of Johnson Creek joins the southern branch. Vale is one of several parks following these streams down Sexton and Cooper mountains. This location provides the opportunity to walk through a small meadow to explore a pond's edge. A short path is flanked by a pair of tall native willows. Around the pond, large Douglas-firs and Oregon ash provide afternoon shade for red and blue dragonflies, fish, and large (noisy) frogs. A Great Blue Heron may be seen, solitary, in the water. In the trees, a Downy Woodpecker may be heard, keeping the beat for the songs of American Robins and Steller's Jays.

The meadow is mostly short grasses and common clovers, with some bird's-foot trefoil and other interesting wildflowers including five-finger (cinquefoil). Some blackberry bushes offer food for robins and jays, as well as starlings and a House Finch. The owner of a house overlooking the pond says she has seen beaver, muskrat, and nutria, as well as raccoons, deer, and garter snakes, in the meadow.

Directions: From Murray Boulevard turn west on Hart Road, left onto SW 149th Avenue. Turn right onto SW Gearhart Drive and stop at the bottom of the hill. A paved path will lead you between houses down to a pond.

Lowami Hart Woods Park.
Photo by Brian Wegener

LOWAMI HART WOODS PARK

Fringe-cups.
Photo by Susan Peter

In 1995, Tualatin Hills Park and Recreation District acquired this site from the Camp Fire organization. Here, just north of Hart Road, Johnson Creek is sheltered by almost 28 acres of Douglas-fir forest that is interlaced with trails established over decades by young campers.

Two miles of unpaved trails meander through a cool, lush forest of ferns and mosses, Oregon-grape, and salal. In May, patches of starflower bloom.

Farther down the slope, fringe-cups grow under service berry bushes, which in turn are shaded by Oregon ash. Beaver live here, not far from a lovely little tree-sheltered meadow; beaver ponds, in time, become meadows. Buttercups and lady ferns are found under the vine maples that stretch and drape their branches over the water and the rocky creek bed. A tributary from the Carolwood neighborhood streams down the eastern slope. Delightfully, even in high summer, Johnson Creek has enough water to be a babbling brook for much of its course through the park.

There are plenty of common, forest-dwelling birds here, but in dense woods it is often easier to identify birds by sound than by sight. The Black-capped Chickadee has one of the easiest calls to recognize. Listen for its "chica-dee-dee-dee." Flickers are also easy to identify with their loud "key-yeer," and Spotted Towhees call their own names: "tow-weeeee." Red-breasted Nuthatches sound like a tiny car alarm, with a repetitive "enk-enk-enk-enk" call.

A large attractive clearing where the old camp headquarters once stood is now a perfect picnic site. Here also is a stout old bridge for those reluctant to cross on the rocks. North of the bridge, look for large avens and two kinds of plantain: English (black) plantain, with its long narrow leaves and halo of teensy white flowers, and broad-leaved plantain, with its nubby green flower stalk. The trail to the Hart Road entrance is lined with duckfoot and waterleaf.

Directions: From SW Murray Boulevard turn west on Hart Road. Right on 152nd. Right on Barcelona Way. A Tualatin Hills Park and Recreation District sign marks a narrow dirt path in the 15100 block. As the path enters the woods, take the right fork to the main trail. The left fork leads only to Johnson Creek. Hart Road entrance has no parking yet. The Tri-Met bus #88 stops here.

Amenities:

83

5 BROOKHAVEN PARK

AREA 5: Beaverton's Johnson Creek

Northern Flicker in nest hole.
Photo by Jim Cruce
"The flicker has an elaborate vocabulary; no other woodpecker, and few other birds, can produce a greater variety of loud striking calls and soft conversational notes." —— Arthur C. Bent, from *Life Histories of North American Woodpeckers*

These 14.5 acres are contiguous with Lowami Hart Woods, but this park is very different. As in the previous park, a tall second-growth forest of Douglas-fir shades the hillsides and a small stream flows from the east to join Johnson Creek. But the bottomland here is mostly natural ponds with just a hint of a free-flowing stream. A wide asphalt path with two bridges connects the two park entrances and, on the hilltop in the southwest corner, there are a few well-maintained bark-chip side trails. The swampy lowland discourages additional trails, but the bridges provide a premier opportunity for waterfowl viewing and spotting freshwater mammals.

Along the paved trail is good birdwatching. You may see, or hear, a Northern Flicker as it taps out a nesting hole or an insect meal. There are Steller's Jays, Western Scrub-Jays, and Red-breasted Nuthatches, as well as Bushtits, chickadees, and if you are lucky, a Brown Creeper.

The Douglas-fir and Oregon ash form a canopy here, with a good variety of understory plants including hazel, Oregon-grape, black hawthorn, and sword fern, but watch out for poison oak. Remember the rhyme: "Leaves of three, let it be!" The three round-lobed leaflets are usually shiny and may show some red throughout the spring and summer; in the fall they are a beautiful scarlet. Even its bare winter branches are poisonous. If you do touch poison oak, wash as soon as you can with soap and water to clean off the oils.

Bushtit. *Photo by Michael Wilhelm*

Directions: From SW Murray Boulevard (see map on page 79) just south of Allen Boulevard, turn west onto Kilchis. Left onto Nehalem. Find a path between 6540 and 6560 SW Nehalem.
Alternate access: West off SW Murray Boulevard onto Hart Road. Right onto 152nd, right onto Barcelona Way. The unmarked entrance between 15056 and 15048 SW Barcelona Way leads to Brookhaven Park. (The marked entrance in the 15100 block leads to Lowami Hart Woods Park.)

Amenities:

6 LILLY K. JOHNSON PARK

While Johnson Creek is not found on this property, it is nearby, and there is a very small rivulet flowing across the back half of this nicely forested little natural area. The apple trees and a few unexpected non-native plants show this to have once been a part of a homestead.

Very large second-growth Douglas-firs provide canopy for most of the park, with the usual understory of small trees and bushes, ground covers, and non-native interlopers. As you follow the barkdust trail deeper into the woods, you may also notice some species that are not commonly found in our small neighborhood parks: red huckleberry, a small Pacific dogwood, mock orange (syringa), salal, and cascara. Red elderberry and young mountain ash add to the dense understory thicket dominated by vine maples. Herbaceous plants include large avens with their prickly little hitchhiking burrs in the summer, yellow wood violets (one of the first flowers in the very early spring), and duckfoot. Duckfoot is also called "inside-out-flower"; both names fit well. Look close to the ground for the one-inch, duck-foot-shaped leaves. In the springtime, notice the backward-turning, creamy white flowers.

Watch for ground-feeding birds such as Dark-eyed Juncos and Spotted Towhees. Bewick's Wrens and Song Sparrows feed in the shrubbery. Nuthatches are the only tree-climbing birds that go down the trunk headfirst; they are small stout birds with strong bills and powerful feet. Look for Red-breasted Nuthatches creeping down Douglas-fir trees in this park. This is also a good place to listen for the Black-capped Chickadees' repetitive call, as well as the harsh shriek of the Western Scrub-Jay.

Towards the back of the park, the canopy is entirely of tall, slender deciduous trees. Then the trail degenerates as the ground drops gently to the tiniest of watercourses. Even in August, the soil here is soft and damp; Oregon ash and willow trees give way, first to a small thicket of steeple bush and wild roses, and then to the grasses and rushes of a small wet meadow. Pretty blue *Veronica* (speedwell) flowers, just 1/2 inch across, and tall, lacy water parsley remind us that the ground here must be flooded much of the year.

Mock orange. *Photo by Susan Peter*

Directions: From Hwy. 217 go west on Farmington Road (Hwy. 10). Turn south on 149th Avenue, right on Division. The Tualatin Hills Park and Recreation sign is in the 15400 block at the crosswalk/speed bump.

Amenities:

AREA 5: Beaverton's Johnson Creek

Insects Along the Tualatin River

By Greg Baker

Choose a sunny summer afternoon for a canoe float down the Tualatin River. Challenge yourself to identify as many types of insects as possible.

Don't be surprised if the first species encountered is the water strider. These spider-like carnivores cruise along the surface in search of tiny springtails, dead "bugs," and emergent insects like mayflies, stoneflies, and midges.

12-spot skimmer

Midges are flies that resemble mosquitoes. However, in our part of the country, most midges do not deliver a bite; nevertheless, unfortunately many get smashed by the uneducated hand.

Up ahead a mayfly survives a gauntlet of striders and fish, only to be taken in flight by a Cedar Waxwing.

A brilliant male twelve-spotted skimmer, or dragonfly, patrols the shore, occasionally resting on a favorite twig. When another dragonfly passes by, the twelve-spot dives from the territorial perch and gives chase to the unwelcome intruder.

Smaller multi-colored damselflies also take wing in search of insect prey. They, in turn, must take evasive actions to avoid falling prey themselves to their larger cousin — the twelve-spotted skimmer.

In an eddy nearby a flotilla of whirligig beetles agitate the surface in what appears to be haphazard motion; however, they are simply covering a lot of area quickly and competing for food.

Suddenly a majestic tiger swallowtail butterfly drifts into view, and then gradually flutters out of sight.

By this time the amateur "bug hunter" may have observed 50 or more insect forms. But as the sun begins to fade we reluctantly add one last species — the pesky mosquito. A good reminder that we have had a wonderful time with the insects on the Tualatin River, and that perhaps it is time to call it a day!

Whirligig beetles

Mayfly

Drawings by
Barbara Macomber

VIEWING AREA 6: Butternut Creek

It is easy to assume that Butternut Creek is yet another part of the extensive Beaverton Creek system. But it is not. It is a primary tributary of the Tualatin River and, once down off the north slope of Cooper Mountain, flows directly west to the river. If you travel out Farmington Road to get to these sites, note that its intersection with Kinnaman Road marks the high point — the divide between Beaverton and Butternut creeks.

Though this is usually a small creek, the intense suburban development in the 1960s and 1970s brought major conflict when roads were repeatedly closed by its floodwaters. More recent development in Washington County reflects the lessons learned here (and elsewhere), including requirements for wetland mitigation plans, surface water management, retention ponds, and opportunities for "planned unit developments" where developers are allowed to build houses on smaller lots in exchange for dedicated streamside parkland.

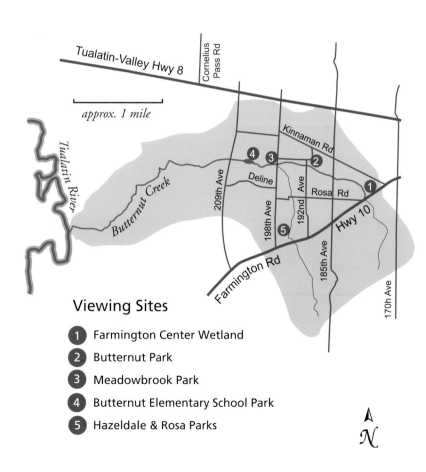

Viewing Sites

1. Farmington Center Wetland
2. Butternut Park
3. Meadowbrook Park
4. Butternut Elementary School Park
5. Hazeldale & Rosa Parks

1 FARMINGTON CENTER WETLAND

This is the main stem of Butternut Creek where it first touches the flatlands. This site would not deserve mention except for the excellent opportunity to view nutria and the damage they do. Towards the far northwest corner of this fenced flood-control pond are a series of nutria dens dug into the mud banks. When water levels are low it is possible not only to view how much erosion is caused by this introduced species, but also to see adult nutria strolling unmolested within their chain link enclave. You might even see the nutria young tussling with each other on the bank in front of the dens. But, note how the plants have been stripped. This wetland was created several years ago, and one would expect mature vegetation, but for too long the plants have provided the main sustenance for the nutria and that has surely taken its toll.

In spite of the scarcity of the vegetation, waterfowl are plentiful here and Mallards and Canada Geese are present throughout the year. American Wigeons may be seen in the late fall and winter. Their other name is "baldpate" because the males' gray heads have shiny white crowns. Their heads also sport a patch of deep glossy green. Both males and females have brown bodies, and it is hard to tell the female wigeons from other female ducks.

Directions: From Highway 217 take Exit 2A. Travel west on Farmington Road (Hwy. 10) 3.3 miles passing 170th Avenue and Kinnaman Road intersections. Turn right into Farmington Center and go to the far west side of the parking lot.

Amenities:

Landing Mallard. *Photo by Jim Cruce*

Colorful Residents of the Tualatin River Basin

American Goldfinch.
Monte Rumgay

Bull thistle.
Susan Peter

Pacific chorus frog. *Michael Wilhem*

Fireweed.
Susan Peter

Western swallowtail.
Steve Berliner

Oregon salamander.
Steve Berliner

Is That a Beaver?

Nutria

Those are most likely nutria, not beaver, swimming in the water. The beaver has a big flat tail, while the nutria's tail is rat-like. Beaver are nocturnal animals, whereas nutria are more likely to be active during the daytime. Nutria were first introduced into the U. S. from South America, where they are known as coypu. Beneath the coarse brown top hair, nutria have a soft dense undercoat and entrepreneurs hoped to get rich breeding them for the fur trade. Unfortunately, when the fur trade collapsed, many nutria were released into streams where, because they are basically herbivorous, the expansion of their population has led to marsh loss. Note: in some places nutria have become "beggars," but please don't encourage these non-native and destructive animals; their long sharp teeth can be dangerous, as well.

Following is a check list to help you identify the nutria and the beaver.

NUTRIA (*Myocastor coypus*)

Description: 2-3 feet long. Tail: Thin, hairy, rat-like, 1 foot long, floats on surface of water. Webbed hind feet. Large, orange, chisel teeth. Outer coat: Reddish-brown. Undercoat: Lighter brown, dense.

Environmental Impact: Erosion caused by burrows and consumption of vegetation on stream banks, lake shores, and marshy areas. Voracious appetite; eat leaves, stems, and roots of marsh grasses and other water plants, leaving nothing for other animals. Prolific: 2-3 litters per year.

Scat: Cylindrical "lozenges" of digested plant material, slippery, dark greenish-black, 2-3 inches long. Usually found along grassy banks and nearby areas. Sometimes seen floating in water.

Tracks: Similar to the beaver's, but usually a bit smaller. Unlike that of the beaver, the nutria's outer toe on the hind foot is not connected to the other toes with webbing. Generally visible because of the small, narrow tail that doesn't obliterate them. Many will be seen together on muddy banks. See below.

Trails: Much the same as a beaver trail, but usually not as wide, and without wood chips and cut trees. They frequently share trails with beavers, so look for their signs: scat and grazed, short-cut grass that appears to be mowed. They also dig channels, and burrow and mine along stream banks.

NUTRIA

BEAVER

4 BUTTERNUT ELEMENTARY SCHOOL PARK

The banks here are low and the water's edge accessible in several spots. Continue downstream through the grass and brush, or use the paved path to get to the far southwest corner of the schoolyard. A passageway between the arching mounds of blackberries leads to a mowed lawn and shady picnic spots. The park ends at an earthen dam and a rocky-bottomed spillway channel in front of a fence. Private property beyond the fence holds another pond before Butternut Creek passes through some more publicly held land at the 209th Avenue sewage pumping station. A half-mile of walking will cover all the trails.

Directions: From Tualatin Valley Highway (Hwy. 8) turn south on 198th Ave.
<u>Access 1:</u> (Best when school is in session) Turn south on 198th Avenue. Turn right on Deline Street. Right on 204th to Jaylee. A narrow path between 20385 and 20415 SW Jaylee leads down the hill.
<u>Access 2:</u> Right on Southview Sreet. Left on 202nd. Down the hill one block and to the right, find a wide pedestrian access to the school. Inside the school ground fence, continue down the hill.

<u>**Amenities:**</u>

Belted Kingfisher (above).

Wood Duck (left).
Photos by Jim Cruce

5 HAZELDALE & ROSA PARKS

Rufous Hummingbird.
Photo by Michael Wilhelm

A small tributary of Butternut Creek sparkles with water all summer long as it courses straight down the north slope of Cooper Mountain and through the 16 acres of these adjoining parks.

A one-mile asphalt pathway starts at Farmington Road and loops past "surface water management" ponds. These ponds collect street runoff and hold it back from the creek until the cat-tails, rushes, sedges, and other natives have had a chance to naturally clean off the worst of the road oils. From 196th Avenue, this trail leads across a footbridge into a patch of oak forest laced with dirt paths for close-up viewing into the stream. The trail continues and makes a large loop around ball fields, tennis courts, and a drinking fountain.

The streamside is shaded by a grove of Oregon white oaks. Under the oaks, snowberry is the most common shrub, but there are several others and there are small spring flowers, too. Look for the purply-pink striped petals of candy flower, a relative of miner's lettuce. Spring beauty, also called small toothwort, is a pale pink member of the Mustard Family. The Mustard Family is characterized by four-petaled flowers, but you may need to spread these tiny cupped blossoms in order to count their petals. In medieval times spring beauty's white, tooth-shaped rhizomes were said to cure toothache. These are early spring flowers, as are the yellow wood violets found here.

Oregon State University researcher Lori Hennings surveyed this park during the spring of 1999. She noted that Rosa Park has a very interesting complex of native shrubs, including twinberry, western wahoo, and red-osier dogwood. During the survey she tallied 27 species of birds. Most were of the common backyard variety, but she also noted among the rich selection of neotropical migrants a Rufous Hummingbird, six Orange-crowned Warblers, a Wilson's Warbler, a Yellow Warbler, a Ruby-crowned Kinglet, and four Warbling Vireos. So take along your bird book, and happy birdwatching!

Directions: From Farmington Road (Hwy. 10) turn north onto 196th Avenue. Hazeldale Park sign is two blocks up on the right. Park on the road.

Amenities:

Candy flower. *Photo by Susan Peter*

A ridge a quarter mile west of the Willamette River defines the watershed between Portland's river and the Tualatin. In the Terwilliger Boulevard area, north of Interstate 5, Fanno Creek starts its journey in the waters of Ivey Creek, passing between Healy Heights and Council Crest. Then Fanno's main channel is seen along Beaverton-Hillsdale Highway (Hwy. 10). Sylvan Creek, which starts just below Skyline Boulevard, crosses under Sunset Highway (U. S. 26) at the Canyon Road exit and parallels Scholls Ferry Road as it comes down from Sylvan. It joins the Fanno Creek mainstem just south of Beaverton-Hillsdale Highway and flows south along Oleson Road. Vermont Creek, coming from the Gabriel Park area, directs the main flow of Fanno Creek again to the west. At Portland Golf Club, Fanno Creek is joined by Woods Creek coming from the southeast. Bearing slightly to the northwest as it again crosses under Scholls Ferry Road, Fanno Creek parallels Allen Boulevard briefly before abruptly turning south and passing under Highway 217. Fanno Creek roughly parallels this freeway, and then I-5, for the rest of its course. (It is, of course, the other way around. Major traffic arteries often follow the flat and level lowland formed by water courses.)

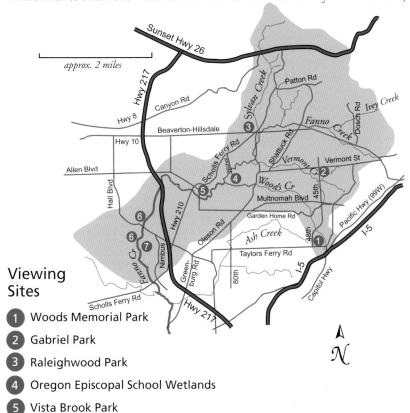

Viewing Sites

1 Woods Memorial Park

2 Gabriel Park

3 Raleighwood Park

4 Oregon Episcopal School Wetlands

5 Vista Brook Park

6 Beaverton's Greenway & Fanno Creek Parks

7 Creekside Marsh

1 WOODS MEMORIAL PARK

Maple with seeds. *Photo by Susan Peter*

This older city park gives one an amazing sense of solitude. It is possible to stand in the middle of Woods Memorial Park and hear nothing but the sound of water, wind through the trees, and an occasional bird. Woods Creek, a tributary of Fanno Creek, can be found down a fairly steep ravine at the very edge of the park.

Leave your car outside the gate and walk along the paved road. On your left are red horsechestnut trees. This is not a native tree, but in May the flower panicles, like fat pink candles, are truly beautiful, and in the fall the green-cased "conkers" are bright and shiny but not edible. On the roadside, among the buttercups and wild strawberries, there are common horsetails. Feel them. The pioneers used these sticky, sandpapery plants for pot scourers.

Just beyond the next gate, on the left, a trail descends through the woods. Look for yellow wood violets in the spring and fringe-cups. Bedstraw or "cleavers" with its sticky leaves has little hooked burrs that cleave to clothes or animal fur. The name "bedstraw" comes from the early English who used the dried plants to stuff mattresses.

This property was logged about 100 years ago. Now, once again, there are some large trees here. Look for the hemlock growing out of the seven-foot-wide cedar stump. Turn the sword fern leaves over to see the "sori." These hold the spores that fulfill the reproductive function of seeds. Look up into the maple trees to find licorice fern, so called because the stems, when chewed, taste faintly like licorice.

If you are lucky you may see Pileated Woodpeckers, Red-winged Blackbirds, Red-tailed Hawks, or Great Blue Herons. Squirrels and raccoons abound. You may even see a coyote.

Down by the creek, you will find lady ferns along with red alders and Indian plum (oso berry). Several trails lead back to the road, and just before you get back to the gate, you'll notice a big meadow. Children love to roll down the slope or blow dandelion puffs while the adults spread a picnic.

Directions: From Portland, southbound on I-5 take Exit 295, Capitol Highway. Turn left at the end of the ramp westbound onto Taylors Ferry Road. Turn right (north) on 48th. Wood Parkway is the second street on the right. The white vehicle gate will probably be closed, but the park is open daily.

Amenities:

2  GABRIEL PARK

Anna's Hummingbird.
Photo by Steve Berliner

AREA 7: Upper Fanno Creek

This 90-acre city park in the rolling hills southwest of Portland provides refuge for some wildlife and many urban-dwelling humans. Vermont Creek once flowed through dairy farms; today the banks have been reclaimed by a forest of Douglas-fir and red-cedar. This tiny stream flows into Fanno Creek and is one of the easternmost tributaries in the Tualatin Basin. Although the understory on the west side of the forest is loved to death by hundreds of daily walkers, an experimental restoration effort is underway. The rest of the park mostly consists of grass-covered hills scattered with a variety of introduced trees. Paved footpaths, changing to gravel in the forest, meander through the park and provide a comfortable walking route.

There are reports of coyotes, raccoons, and other mammals living in the park, but birds are much more commonly encountered. The best places to look for birds are along the edges of the forest and around the wetland area. Year-round you may see: Spotted Towhees, Song Sparrows, Bushtits, Anna's Hummingbirds, Pine Siskins, Golden and Ruby-crowned kinglets, Northern Flickers, Downy Woodpeckers, House Finches, Dark-eyed Juncos, and American Robins. From December to April, the long, loud silvery warble of the Winter Wren can be heard from deep within the forest undergrowth of sword fern and red huckleberry. Bewick's Wrens are also common, but tend to stick to the brushy margins of elderberry, blackberry, and hawthorn where they belt out their "dial five" song from April through June. In the spring and summer, swallows, swifts, flycatchers, and warblers are present. A small wetland restoration project on the east end of the park has successfully attracted a number of species, including Mallards and rusty-voiced Red-winged Blackbirds, and in the winter, flocks of gulls. From mid-March, wildflowers are plentiful. Trilliums, Indian plums (oso berries), and other forest plants are followed in late May by an impressive wall of rhododendrons in the southwest corner of the park.

Directions: From Portland, turn south off Beaverton-Hillsdale Highway (Hwy. 10) at 30th, then right onto Vermont and left onto 42nd. From Beaverton, travel east on Beaverton-Hillsdale Highway, turn south on Oleson Road, then left on Vermont. At 45th Avenue, beyond the large Southwest Community Center building, is the park. Turn right at 42nd to find a parking lot.

Amenities:

AREA 7: Upper Fanno Creek

③ RALEIGHWOOD PARK

Would you like to see what happens when a group of people decides to develop their own small nature park? Students at West Sylvan Middle School, led by their science teacher Joe Blowers (and supported by parents, neighbors, and Fans of Fanno Creek), decided that tiny Sylvan Creek should be improved to become more viable wildlife habitat. Since then, Wood Duck nesting boxes have been installed, and 65 Wood Ducks have been counted. There are year-round Belted Kingfishers, and a winter population of Hooded Mergansers. Great Blue Herons make their homes here. In the brush, juncos, Bewick's Wrens, House Finches, and thrushes carol their presence along with migrating warblers. Northern Flickers and Brown Creepers tap the Douglas-fir and bigleaf maple for insects while Violet-green Swallows swoop overhead. A beaver is building a dam and beaver-chewed young trees are apparent. This partially wooded hillside park looks out over a pond and weeping willow trees.

Directions: This park is on Dogwood Road, which is a minor player in the complex intersection of Beaverton-Hillsdale Highway (Hwy. 10), Scholls Ferry Road (Hwy. 210), and Oleson Road. Best access is from southbound on Scholls Ferry Road. Before actually entering the intersection, keep right, close in front of Parr Lumber. Immediately turn right onto Dogwood, going up a steep hill. Park is on the right.

Amenities:

Oregon Episcopal School Wetlands.
Photo by Brian Wegener

Bittersweet nightshade.
Photo by Susan Peter

AREA 7: Upper Fanno Creek

Fanno Creek Park is a narrow corridor with a wide paved path that follows the somewhat overgrown creek. Thickets of bittersweet nightshade and blackberries are shaded by red-cedar and Oregon ash. There are also some red elderberry trees and English hawthorn; the red berries of both of these are attractive to Cedar Waxwings.

Behind the tangle of vines, a croaking frog signals the presence of wetland. You might see a Great Blue Heron; they are quite common in these wetter areas of the park. The best view is from the bridge just north of Hall Boulevard. On a fall day, a glimpse of the creek shows that it is leaf-choked and slow moving and there are signs here of a busy beaver at work trying to turn the stream into a marsh. A notice board, a little off the trail amid bulrushes and reed canarygrass, points out that the latter was planted by local farmers and later by the predecessors of Clean Water Services to prevent erosion. However, with no control, it has taken over the wetlands that once were covered by tufted hairgrass and camas. Another notice board, this one banning fires, reminds us that the Atfalati, the Native Americans of this area, were careful when they burned the valley floor to leave an unburned strip of woodland along the creek.

Across Hall Boulevard, in **Greenway Park**, the three-mile trail crosses mowed lawns with play equipment for children and a collection of wooden exercise apparatus for adults. Fanno Creek feeds several wetland habitats that are better viewed from the opposite bank. A side trail leads to a bridge across the creek, shaded by red alders and Oregon ash. Follow this side trail to find the historic Fanno Farmhouse, and consider continuing south through the business parks here to view Creekside Marsh. Greenway Park's main trail continues south beyond Scholls Ferry Road into Tigard and gives cyclists, roller-bladers, and the wheelchair-bound a chance to get out and away from motorized vehicles.

Directions: Fanno Creek Park: From Hwy. 217 turn west on Denney Road. Turn left almost immediately into small parking lot at Tualatin Hills Park and Recreation District sign. If you miss this, turn left onto Bel-aire and continue for three blocks. Park at Fanno Street on left.
Greenway Park: From Hall Blvd. turn south onto Greenway Blvd. The Albertsons at the corner is one of many neighborhood access points. A short distance south on Greenway Blvd. a wide arm of the park is visible from the road.

Amenities:

Fanno Creek Park:

Greenway Park:

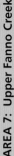

7 CREEKSIDE MARSH

This gem of a viewing area is at the back of a huge office complex. When the site was cleared for building, Douglas-firs, bigleaf maples, and Oregon white oaks were left in place. A fine viewing platform overlooks a marsh, which in the winter becomes a pond.

As well as the ubiquitous Canada Geese and Mallards, there are Green-winged Teals, Northern Pintails, Gadwalls, American Wigeons, and Buffleheads. As the floodwaters recede, yellowlegs, dowitchers, and Common Snipe probe the mudflats for insects and worms. Red-winged Blackbirds call from the bushes. In a Douglas-fir, and within plain sight of the covered platform, a Great Blue Heron tends her fluffy chick. By May, the calls of hungry baby herons ring over the noise of the traffic on busy Hall Boulevard. By summer, cat-tail, bulrush, sedge, and reed canarygrass fill the marsh, cleaning polluted water before it reaches nearby Fanno Creek. Both the pond and the creek itself have river otters as well as (non-native) snapping turtles.

The bird list includes Virginia Rails, American Bitterns, owls, Red-tailed Hawks, Great Egrets, Belted Kingfishers, Downy and Pileated woodpeckers, Spotted Towhees, Song Sparrows, Bewick's Wrens, Northern Flickers, Band-tailed Pigeons, and Mourning Doves. There are wildflowers aplenty including fairy lantern, twisted-stalk, and large false Solomon's seal. In the fall, the pond refills with water, the plants die back, and the winter migrants return.

Directions: Southbound on Highway 217 take Progress exit. West on Hall Blvd., over railway, left on Nimbus. Turn right on Gemini Drive, then right into first parking lot. West across the parking lot see the roof of the viewing platform. The marsh can also be viewed from parking lots north and south of here. Northbound on Highway 217 take Scholls Ferry Road exit, turn right. Turn left at Hall Boulevard and follow directions above.

Amenities:

Common Snipe.
Photo by Jim Cruce

VIEWING AREA 8: Lower Fanno Creek

Fanno Creek enters Tigard much as it left Beaverton: surrounded by parkland. An unnamed tributary from the west joins it in Englewood Park. The wetlands seen from Highway 217 just south of Washington Square are part of Ash Creek, which, continuing west of the highway, flows under Greenburg Road to enter the main stem. Summer Creek flows eastward passing through Fowler Junior High playing fields before joining Fanno Creek. Through the center of historic Tigard, Fanno Creek is again surrounded by expansive natural parkland. Red Rock Creek, also seen from Highway 217, adds to the flow just downstream from the Tigard Library. South of Bonita Road near 74th Street, Fanno Creek is greeted by the Ball/Carter Creek system, which starts in west Lake Oswego and the Kruse Way area. As Fanno Creek continues paralleling 72nd Street, it flows under Durham Road and into Durham City Park. Here, it joins the Tualatin River.

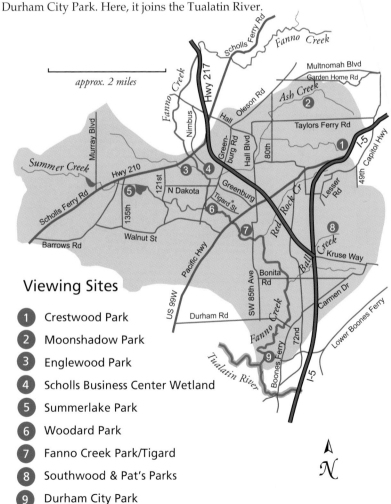

Viewing Sites

1. Crestwood Park
2. Moonshadow Park
3. Englewood Park
4. Scholls Business Center Wetland
5. Summerlake Park
6. Woodard Park
7. Fanno Creek Park/Tigard
8. Southwood & Pat's Parks
9. Durham City Park

1 CRESTWOOD PARK

Crestwood Park on the south fork of Ash Creek offers a steep trail, somewhat rough and not suitable for the less-agile, but pleasantly winding through bigleaf maple, Douglas-fir, and red-cedar. Where trees have been logged off, volunteers have been busy planting both replacement forest trees and native shrubs. In spite of its proximity to I-5, Crestwood is home to Red-tailed Hawks, Pileated Woodpeckers, and more common birds such as sparrows, Spotted Towhees, House Finches, Western Scrub- and Steller's jays, and noisy ravens. Squirrels chatter from the tree branches and there are raccoons.

Directions: From Portland, Barbur Boulevard to Taylors Ferry Road, right on Taylors Ferry, left on 53rd all the way to the end of the road. There are no signs, and due to its steepness, the trail will not be visible from your car.

Amenities:

Red-tailed Hawk.
Photo by Jim Cruce

Spotted Towhee.
Photo by Jim Cruce

2 MOONSHADOW PARK

Clearly, the residents of the nearby houses agree that this strip of wilderness along Ash Creek is worth preserving. The park is owned by the Tualatin Hills Park and Recreation District, but the homeowners built the sturdy wooden bridge to replace one that had washed away during the 1996 floods and they keep a close eye on the park and its flora and fauna.

As one walks down the smooth asphalt trail, recent streamside plantings of young trees and shrubs, including hemlocks and snowberries, are further evidence of these neighborhood efforts, which have also extended to trying to control the pesky blackberries (an ongoing problem).

Mature trees include red-cedar, Oregon ash, red alder, Indian plum, vine maple, bigleaf maple, and Douglas-fir. There is one large old, fire-scarred Douglas-fir which is estimated to be at least 600 years old, but which unfortunately lost its top some 16 years ago, and is slowly dying. The Pileated Woodpeckers have made good use of it as their own "condo" as well as a source of insects.

Along with the masses of Himalayan and evergreen blackberries and the snowberries are red elderberries, wild roses, and bittersweet nightshade vines. Horsetails, bracken, and sword fern all grow amid a wild garden rich in color and variety. A patch of spearmint has become naturalized and gives off its chewing-gum scent underfoot.

As well as the Pileated Woodpeckers, there are American Robins, Western Scrub-Jays and Steller's Jays, Black-capped Chickadees, House Finches, Common Ravens, and at least one owl. Even an occasional Great Blue Heron visits the creek. Although the Mallards do nest here, they never manage to rear their ducklings due to the proliferation of neighborhood cats. Frogs and crawfish both thrive in the creek, and raccoons have been spotted as well as coyotes. After dark, there are bats.

Wild rose.
Photo by Susan Peter

Directions: From Oleson Road take Garden Home Road east, and stay straight on Garden Home Road (do not take Multnomah). Turn south on 62nd Avenue, then right on Dolph Drive. Turn right again on Alden. You will see a signed entrance along here, or you can go on to the Alden Court entrance.

Amenities:

③ ENGLEWOOD PARK

This 15-acre park has two trails, each through a somewhat different habitat. One is on the floodplain of Fanno Creek, the other along a small tributary. These trails do not connect within the park, but the connection can easily be made by walking a short distance along Ironwood Drive. Although not labeled as such in the park, for clarity here we refer to them as the Cedar Grove Trail and the Fanno Floodplain Trail.

Cedar Grove Trail: From Hazelwood Loop access, a trail leads to a bridge over this small tributary of Fanno Creek. Note the very healthy red alder shading the water; its long, green catkins have already formed by November. Alders fix nitrogen into the soil, promoting a rich undergrowth of grasses, sedges, and ferns. Beyond the bridge is a children's playground. Go back along the main trail. On the left, Himalayan blackberry is rampant; on the right are mowed lawns and a row of tall poplar trees.

Cross Springwood Road and stay on the upper, right-hand trail, still paralleling the creek. Soon the sweet smell of cedar is in the air. To the left, a partially dead cedar tree provides a playground for two squirrels. See how it is riddled with woodpecker holes. As you enter the cedar grove, pause a moment and enjoy the quiet. These are western red-cedars, the trees most prized by the Native Americans of the Pacific Northwest. They furnished wood for canoes, house planks, and posts. The roots made baskets, the beaten bark was fashioned into clothing.

There are bigleaf maples here too, and under the canopy, sword ferns flourish. Just before the solid little bridge is a patch of skunk cabbage. The little creek flows swiftly here, through banks lined with Indian plum (oso berry), blackberries, and bittersweet nightshade.

Over the bridge, the trail divides. One route leads past a playground and back to Springwood Drive; the other goes up a slight incline to Ironwood Drive. If you wish to connect to the Fanno Floodplain Trail from here, turn right to walk down Ironwood Drive for about 0.1 mile to the next park access. It is on the right. This will take you into a very different habitat midway along the Fanno Floodplain Trail. Before reaching the main trail, you will see a children's play area with a picnic table.

Hazel has a velvety soft leaf surface with finely toothed edges.

Red alder has doubly serrated edges.

Fanno Floodplain Trail: This is a downstream extension of Beaverton's Greenway Park Trail, to which it is linked by a rather spooky pedestrian underpass at Scholls Ferry Road. If you enter from the path next to 11338 Ironwood Drive, turn right. To the left there is a view of the Scholls Business Center Wetland (see page 112). Reed canarygrass rules here, but the indefatigable Fans of Fanno Creek have planted young maples, red-cedars, red-osier (creek) dogwoods, wild roses, red alders, and ninebark bushes.

Common horsechestnut. *Photo by Susan Peter*

Farther down the trail, notice how Himalayan blackberry is out of control, climbing high up trees. However, several kinds of wild roses are holding their own, and in the fall the birds enjoy the red hips. A trail to the right passes a children's play area with a picnic table. Take a moment to sit, look, and listen. The black locust tree, an import from the Midwest, has golden leaves in the fall, but in the spring the white flowers are fragrant. There are Dark-eyed Juncos in the young lodgepole pines. A Northern Flicker comes down from a tree to peck in the grass. The main trail passes over a culvert where the tributary described under "Cedar Creek Trail" joins Fanno Creek. Reed canarygrass dominates both sides of the trail, but it continues to offer glimpses of Fanno Creek as it meanders south.

At South Dakota Street the trail seems to end. But walk right. Notice the chestnut trees in the apartment grounds. The prickly burrs hold the tiny, sweet nuts. Cross the street. Fanno Creek is now far to the left sheltered by Oregon ash and a few Douglas-fir. The trail ends at Tigard Street. In the garden of the older home to your right are fine grape vines, and there is a horsechestnut tree in front. In the spring, its ruffled white flowers look like tiny orchids; in the fall, the ground is covered with shiny nuts which are not edible. Next to the house is a windmill that once pumped water to the residents. To the left, a bridge offers a glimpse of the creek.

There are plenty of birds on this section of the trail, but you may hear more than you see. On a sunny November day, a Red-tailed Hawk flies lazily over the wetlands. There are both Scrub-Jays and Steller's Jays, and a flock of American Crows settles noisily into a maple tree.

<u>**Directions:**</u> From Highway 217 go west on Scholls Ferry Road 0.6 miles and turn left on Springwood Drive. <u>Fanno Floodplain Trail:</u> turn left on Ironwood Loop. Paved path enters park next to 11338 Ironwood. <u>Cedar Grove Trail:</u> turn right on Hazelwood Loop. Access path is next to 11575 Hazelwood.

<u>**Amenities:**</u>

4 SCHOLLS BUSINESS CENTER WETLAND

Here, behind Scholls Business Park, the Fans of Fanno Creek have created an attractive wetland park. They have planted steeple bush, Douglas-fir, red-osier dogwood, red-cedar and Oregon ash and have left large snags in place to attract Bald Eagles and other birds that perch high to watch for prey. Wood Ducks like to nest high, and nesting boxes have been placed to attract these, our most ducks. Great Blue Herons also nest high up in trees and can be seen wading in the marshy water.

Mallards like it here. Also, watch for Common Mergansers; the males have green-black heads, black backs and white bodies, and the gray females have crested reddish-brown heads and white underparts.

This is part of a series of protected areas along Fanno Creek. See sites on pages 103, 107 and 110.

<u>**Directions:**</u> From Highway 217 go west on Scholls Ferry Road, crossing the railroad tracks. On the left, Nimbus Drive enters the Scholls Business Center. You can view the wetlands on the right-hand side beyond the directory board.

Evergreen blackberry has lacy deeply divided leaves. Although a non-native, it is not as large or aggressive as the Himalayan blackberry.

Himalayan blackberry has a palmate leaf. It is an invasive non-native with large arching maroon-tinted canes that create unwelcome thickets.

Trailing blackberry (dewberry) is a native, low-growing creeper. A bluish blush often coats its slender canes.

5 SUMMERLAKE PARK

AREA 8: Lower Fanno Creek

Lupine and California poppies.
Photo by Susan Peter

Summerlake Park offers bosky trails with a variety of trees and wildflowers, a lake which is home to numerous waterfowl and aquatic animals, and a paved trail which circles the lake, following its undulating and varied shoreline. From the parking lot, a paved path leads to a bridge and a picnic shelter. Notice the water-loving blue *Veronica*, water-cress, red sorrel, sedge, and duckweed. There are also black-eyed Susans, evening primrose, yellow-gold California poppy, and two kinds of *Clarkia*.

A soft path leads from the playground, and you may see Steller's and Western Scrub-Jays, American Crows, Song and House sparrows, Dark-eyed Juncos, and American Robins in the woods, but on reaching the lake, the birding gets much more interesting. Here, Vaux's Swifts and Barn Swallows perform aerial ballets, a Belted Kingfisher dives for fish, Mallards, Canada Geese, and a Pied-billed Grebe swim by, and a Green Heron darts out from the reed canarygrass. A solitary Great Blue Heron stands tall.

Returning through the woods, we identify Douglas-fir, red-osier dogwood, oceanspray, cascara, and a huge red-cedar nurse tree with two young trees growing on its remains. Among the velvety leaves of the hazels are young green nuts, but this is July; by late fall most will have been eaten. As a Douglas squirrel chatters to us from a nearby tree, we move back to the footpath to notice some of the wildflowers growing there. Steeple bush, trailing blackberry, and Oregon-grape are all indigenous, but Scotch broom, Himalayan and evergreen blackberry, English holly, and English hawthorn are less desirable introduced species.

Before we leave, we notice a horde of European Starlings wheeling overhead. These immigrants can drive out native birds and greedily devour fruits such as cherries and apples. Since they can have as many as three broods a year, the size of flocks rapidly increases so that thousands of European Starlings can invade a neighborhood, an orchard, or a farmer's field.

Directions: From Scholls Ferry Road, turn south on SW 130th Avenue which becomes SW Winter Lake Drive.

Amenities:

6 WOODARD PARK

Oregon-grape.
Photo by Susan Peter

Little Woodard Park still hints at what it was like when once-wild Fanno Creek flowed through green fields before the houses and apartment buildings crowded in.

There are Oregon white oaks; notice the "oak apples," not a fruit, but a round gall. These galls are growths caused by the parasitic gall wasp. There is a small grove of Douglas-fir; see the pretty, spear-shaped seeds tucked into the cones. When children are taught to identify these seeds, they are often told to look for the little tails and hind legs of tiny mice hiding in the cone. Then, look at the prickly cones of the sole ponderosa pine. Its long, dark green needles are always in bundles of three.

Oregon-grape, wild rose, and Indian plum (oso berry) crowd the creek banks. Indian plum, with its simple leaves, is common in the understory of most of our forests. Late February is a good time to look for it, as it is the first to leaf out in the spring. A little wooden bridge close to the Johnson Street entrance must have been designed for playing "Pooh Sticks": dropping sticks off one side of the bridge and watching as they come out on the other side.

On a rainy March day, few birds were in evidence. Certainly there were Western Scrub-Jays and Steller's Jays and Common Ravens overhead. Perhaps, on a sunny day, this is a place to take a child or two, to play on the swings and enjoy a picnic snack. You can tell the legend of Raven, how he stole the old man's treasure box, released the stars, moon, and sun, and brought light to the world. Not a bad way to spend an hour or so.

Directions: From Highway 217 take the Tigard exit. Head southwest on Pacific Highway (US 99W). After the Tigard overpass, immediately turn right onto Johnson Street. Woodard Park is on the right where the street curves.

Amenities:

Sharp-shinned
Hawk.
*Photo by
Jim Cruce*

7 FANNO CREEK PARK/TIGARD

This urban greenspace located right behind Tigard's City Hall and Library supports a surprisingly wide variety of wildlife. So, start your trip at the library, where you can check out bird and wildflower field guides. Ask for a copy of the Tualatin Riverkeepers' bird list, *Birds of the Lower Tualatin River*.

Go to the back of the library and notice the bird feeder which serves a fluttering bevy of sparrows, finches, juncos, towhees, and chickadees. Then, go on down the trail to the pond. Mallards live here year-round, but winter is really the best time to see waterbirds. Winter visitors include Hooded Mergansers; the male sports a spectacular white crest which he habitually raises, and the female has a tawny head and dark crest.

Following the trail round the pond, notice the plantings of Oregon-grape and snowberry, as well as the thickets of invasive Himalayan blackberries. Continue east to Hall Boulevard and cross it to see a wetland and pond that is visited regularly by Canada Geese, Belted Kingfishers, and Great Blue Herons. Occasionally there is also a less common visitor such as a Great Egret.

Now head back west along the trail. Check out the views of the creek from the bridges made from old flatbed railroad cars. Keep your eye out for colorful Wood Ducks and Green Herons and notice the Oregon white oaks that play host to jays, woodpeckers, and Sharp-shinned Hawks. There are songbirds in the blackberry brambles and Red-winged Blackbirds can be seen (and heard) in open areas along the creek.

In summer, a side trip over the first bridge reveals a spectacular display of wild roses and, in May, the showy white flowers of the black hawthorn decorate the trail.

The wetland extends along the creek up to the back of the businesses on Main Street. Several side trails lead to different neighborhoods, but as yet, direct access to Main Street is blocked; however, if you do go to Main Street, you can see where Fanno Creek passes under the road. Eventually, Fanno Creek Park in Tigard will be a major component of the Fanno Creek Trail, a walking and bicycle path that will link Tigard, Beaverton, and Portland.

Directions: From Pacific Highway (US 99W), turn south onto Hall Boulevard (85th Avenue) for 0.7 mile to the Tigard Public Library and City Hall. The park entrance is in the Tigard Civic Center between City Hall and the library.

Amenities:

8 SOUTHWOOD & PAT'S PARKS

These little parks on Ball Creek offer a peek at a small tributary of Fanno Creek hidden in a forest of Douglas-fir, vine maple, and bigleaf maple. Hazels provide part of the understory. In the fall, hazelnuts provide food for squirrels; in the spring the male flowers, the catkins, appear before the leaves. See if you can find female catkins; they are very small and have protruding red stigmas. Hazelnuts were enjoyed by the Atfalati, the first people of the Tualatin. They also used the young branches, which are flexible enough to be twisted into rope.

Along the stream are red alder and willow. Next to the trail are red-flowering currants, wood violets, wild strawberries, and herb-Robert — a tiny relative of the geranium with a name so ancient no one now knows which of several famous Roberts is honored. There is also at least one patch of kinnikinnick (bearberry). Although the word "kinnikinnick" is Algonquin, the leaves of this plant were also smoked, either alone or mixed with tobacco, by a number of native Northwest tribes.

There are several little paths leading off the main trail. Towards the north end of the park where several streams converge, a flood control dam creates a small bog. Listen for the "chick-a-dee-dee-dee" call of the Black-capped Chickadees, the buzzing of Bewick's Wrens, and the high-pitched, repetitive "tsee-tsee-tsee" of the Golden-crowned Kinglets. Often you can bring these small birds to within a few feet of you by making a repeated "psh-psh-psh" sound.

Directions: From Pacific Highway (99W) in Tigard, east of Highway 217, turn south on SW 68th Avenue. Then turn left on SW Haines/Atlanta Street over I-5. Turn south on Lesser Road to 62nd Avenue (a tricky little intersection). Follow 62nd south 0.8 miles to the corner of Pamela. Park on the street.

Amenities:

Durham City Park Bridge.
Photo by Brian Wegener

9 | DURHAM CITY PARK

AREA 8: Lower Fanno Creek

Here, where Fanno Creek empties into the Tualatin River, the flora and fauna typical of upland forest, riparian woodland, freshwater wetland, and winter-flooded fields can be found in season. In winter, a sizeable flock of mixed dabbling geese and ducks, chiefly Canada Geese, American Wigeons, and Green-winged Teals, can be found. Mixed among them are Northern Pintails, usually some Eurasian Wigeons, and Mallards. Hooded Mergansers, Buffleheads, Lesser Scaups, and Pied-billed Grebes also occur. Pileated Woodpeckers, Ospreys, Belted Kingfishers, and Great Blue Herons breed in the area.

Other wildlife also enjoy the park. There is an active coyote den somewhere in this area. Early spring brings out droves of night-calling male chorus frogs. Garter snakes are plentiful in the meadow areas.

Lesser Scaup (above). Northern Pintails (left). *Photos by Jim Cruce*

While there are both deciduous and coniferous trees throughout the park, two imports stand out. Behind the play area, note the stand of purple beeches, and along the trails in the spring the English hawthorn displays its showy, creamy white flowers. Its deeply-lobed leaves distinguish it from the native black hawthorn. Note, too, the native trailing blackberries. Their young stems are aqua blue and the berries ripen earlier than the more plentiful Himalayan blackberries. See if you can also find another import, the evergreen blackberry, with its deeply incised and finely toothed leaves. See page 112.

Close to Fanno Creek, look for other introduced species. The pretty yellow bird's-foot trefoil, a member of the Pea Family, decorates the grassy verges of the stream, while in nearby meadows purple self-heal (its square stem reminds you it is a member of the Mint Family) and ox-eye daisy delight the eye.

Directions: I-5 to Exit 291. Turn west and follow signs for King City. Turn left to go south on Upper Boones Ferry Road past Durham Road. Turn right on SW Rivendell Drive (a loop), then right down SW Arkenstone to the park entrance.

Ox-eye daisies. *Photo by Susan Peter*

Amenities:

A Walk in the Park

By Thomas Love,
Professor of Anthropology, Linfield College

Northern Shovelers.
Photo by Jim Cruce

Itook a short walk with my two boys late Saturday morning in Durham Park. This is where Fanno Creek empties into the Tualatin River. The City of Durham, which incorporated to "oppose progress," is sandwiched between Tigard and Tualatin. Durham's City Park forms the eastern part of a relatively large open space which includes Tigard's more developed Cook Park and Tualatin's somewhat less developed Community Park. Right in the center of all this is the Thomas Dairy. Clean Water Services recently acquired the dairy and is working with Metro and the City of Tigard to allocate this flooded field (formerly floodplain/wetland) into a picnic area, wetlands, and trails. It holds a lot of potential, particularly as the wetlands are restored.

At the edge of the woods we saw a Pileated Woodpecker working a snag. Recently arrived Pine Siskins worked the tips of deciduous trees along the creek. Farther along, out to the eastern edge of the dairy's flooded fields, we disturbed a typical wintering flock of dabbling ducks, including at least 80 American Wigeon and over 200 Green-winged Teal, with a few Northern Shovelers and Mallards. (There is often a Eurasian Wigeon in this flock, and I have seen Hooded Merganser in a nearby mitigation pond.) Also in the flooded south part of the Thomas Dairy property was the usual wintering flock of about 40 Canada Geese.

But most unusual was the one Snow Goose in with the others, grinning patch and all. All of a sudden the ducks and geese flushed. I felt bad, thinking we had come too close and scared them all off. Then I looked up and there was an adult Bald Eagle, which made a long sweeping pass over the area and then headed on down the Tualatin.

Nice birds for a local city park on a gray winter day!

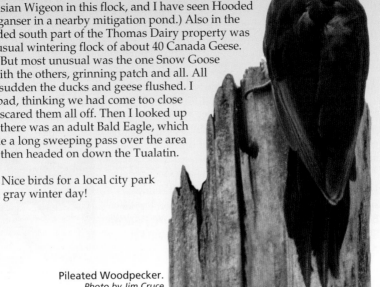

Pileated Woodpecker.
Photo by Jim Cruce

VIEWING AREA 9: Lower Tualatin River (West of I-5)

The southwest portion of the Tualatin River watershed is mostly farmland (flatland and hillside orchards) and the wooded slopes of the mountains that form its boundary with the Yamhill River watershed. Chehalem Mountain is a long ridge whose high point at 1,629 feet is known as Bald Peak. The north end of this ridge extends into the heart of the Tualatin Valley, sending western creeks towards Gaston and the river's headwaters; northern creeks toward Forest Grove and Hillsboro; and eastern creeks toward the tiny farm communities of Laurel, Farmington, Midway, and Scholls. Davis, Christensen, Burris, McFee, Heaton, Baker, and Chicken creeks are the largest ones draining the near slope of Chehalem Mountain.

Farther east, Cedar Creek shares the right of way with Highway 99 West as they slip between Chehalem and Parrett mountains. Cedar Creek then flows through Sherwood's Stella Olsen Park before joining Chicken Creek and the river. Rock Creek forms on Pleasant Hill. Onion Flat near Cipole Road, like Wapato Lake near Gaston, is a seasonal lake and was an important source of wapato tubers for the Atfalati tribes. Little Hedges Creek begins near Avery Street and Boones Ferry Road.

Left bank tributaries between Butternut Creek (draining the Aloha area) and Fanno Creek (draining Portland's southwest neighborhoods, South Beaverton, and Tigard) are minimal. The largest, sometimes known as Tile Flat Creek since it flows along Tile Flat Road, drains the south slope of Cooper Mountain.

The Tualatin River is typical of a mature streambed with meanders and oxbow lakes. Thick streamside vegetation helps to restrain some of the river's natural tendency toward side-cutting of the banks. This conserves farmland and reduces silting of the water. Riparian trees shade the water to keep it cool for native fish. The new Tualatin River National Wildlife Refuge is currently a patchwork of 1,000 acres committed to this type of high-quality streamside; some of these acres are already in native vegetation while others are being replanted and restored.

Metro is committed to providing public access every five to seven miles along the Tualatin River, and funds from the 1995 Metro Open Space Parks and Stream bond measure are being used for this purpose. Watch for details in new editions of the *Tualatin River Paddling Guide* published by The Tualatin Riverkeepers.

Cooper Mountain Preserve (see page 122). *Photo by Susan Peter*

VIEWING AREA 9: Lower Tualatin River (West of I-5)

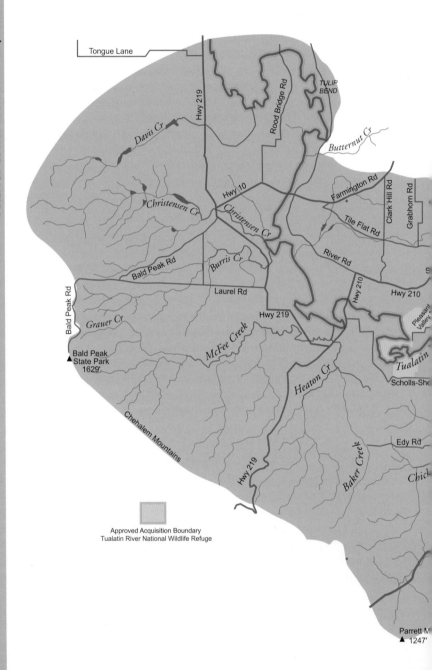

Approved Acquisition Boundary
Tualatin River National Wildlife Refuge

VIEWING AREA 9: Lower Tualatin River (West of I-5)

Viewing Sites

1. Cooper Mountain Preserve
2. Tualatin River National Wildlife Refuge
3. Stella Olsen Memorial Park & Cedar Creek Greenway
4. Ibach Park & Upper Hedges Creek Greenway
5. Little Wood Rose Nature Park
6. Hedges Creek Marsh
7. Apache Bluff Wetland
8. Cook Park
9. Tualatin Community Park

1 COOPER MOUNTAIN PRESERVE

The southward view from this preserve is spectacular. As you look beyond the Tualatin River, which meanders out of sight, you may be able to identify Parrett Mountain as the rounded shape in the far distance and Chehalem Mountain as the ridge to the southwest.

Cooper Mountain is one of several shield volcanoes forming the Tualatin Valley, and while the valley floor is deep alluvial soils, here the bedrock of vesicular (holey) lava is exposed along the roadway. The mountain's thin soil, which is unable to retain much moisture, together with the elevation, slope, and southern exposure, creates a radically different vegetation and wildlife habitat from that of lowland and riparian zones. The summer wildflowers tend to be drought resistant: goldenrod, yarrow, honeysuckle, pearly everlasting, and great mullein. Tall purple Douglas' asters grow well here, as does St. John's wort, a tall plant with tiny yellow flowers that are miniatures of the garden variety ground cover. Hold one of the little leaves up to the light and see the pinholes that give them their Latin name, *Hypericum perforatum*.

The trail into the preserve is an old, unpaved road. In late spring the brilliant yellow of our state flower, the Oregon-grape, competes with the gold of the Scotch broom. Delight in the exuberant red-flowering currant and the little white wild strawberry flowers. Beyond the small plaque commemorating Metro's acquisition of the park, the trail splits. Go to the right, then take the left-hand road. Up on the bank, just before reaching the old quarry, is one of several nesting boxes designed to meet the specific needs of the Western Bluebird. This little bird has a thin bill, a blue head and wings, and a rusty red breast. Though it was once quite common, the loss of natural nesting cavities, such as dead trees and wooden fence posts, and competition from non-native house sparrows and starlings, forced it out of this part of Oregon. Today, thanks to volunteers from the Hubert Prescott Western Bluebird Recovery Project who set up and monitor these boxes, the Western Bluebird is making a recovery. In late spring and early summer, watch the adult birds as they fly in and out of the nests to feed their young.

Western Bluebird nesting box at Cooper Mountain Preserve. *Photo by Susan Peter*

Cooper Mountain Preserve is great bird habitat. On a single March day, our birders identified 22 different species of birds, including five kinds of sparrows. You may need a

2 TUALATIN RIVER NATIONAL WILDLIFE REFUGE

The Tualatin River National Wildlife Refuge is located between King City, Sherwood, and Scholls. Currently the refuge consists of just over 1,000 acres of permanent ponds, seasonal wetlands, riparian forests, and upland habitats. Eventually the refuge will cover 3,058 acres as land is acquired from willing sellers. Future development will include a visitors' center, wildlife viewing facilities, and river access.

At this time, the refuge is closed to public access except for special events run by the Friends of the Refuge. The two biggest events of the year are the International Migratory Songbird Festival in May and Refuge Appreciation Week in October. During these events, the Friends lead bird walks through the various habitats and the Tualatin Riverkeepers lead canoe trips on the river. At several other times of the year, the Friends lead bird walks with local birding groups such as Audubon Society of Portland. Seasonal highlights to watch for on the refuge include waterfowl in the winter, neotropical migratory songbirds in the spring, and shorebirds at the end of summer. Permanent residents include Bald Eagles and a variety of wading birds.

Volunteer opportunities with the Friends include leading tours, special events, wildlife surveys, and restoration planting projects. For more information about refuge access, events and tours, or volunteer opportunities, contact the Friends of the Refuge at 503-972-7714.

Friends of the Refuge/Audubon Society of Portland field trip to the Tualatin River National Wildlife Refuge, August 1999. *Photo by Brian Wegener*

AREA 9: Lower Tualatin River (West of I-5)

The eight-acre Stella Olsen Park is now part of the City of Sherwood's 100-acre Cedar Creek Greenway. The park is centered on two islands created by the meandering channels of Cedar Creek. Children will enjoy the wildlife, as well as the new playground equipment. An occasional squirrel forages under the Douglas-firs, red-cedars, and maples. Along the creek, Mallards swim beneath the alders and willows. Towhees, robins, jays, juncos, chickadees, several kinds of sparrows, and ravens are all plentiful.

Those seeking a more interesting ecological environment should take the connecting trail along Cedar Creek. Here, despite its proximity to the city, the greenway has remained relatively undeveloped and the variety of plants, birds, and mammals is impressive. There are coyotes, deer, beaver, raccoons, and squirrels as well as the non-native nutria, a residual from once-profitable fur farms. Along with the common songbirds, Bald Eagles, Red-tailed Hawks, and a Great Horned Owl have been spotted. One can also see Pileated Woodpeckers, flycatchers, several species of warblers, Brown Creepers, and many duck species. There are crawfish in the creek. In the spring, a patch of marsh is resplendent with yellow spathes hooding the spikes of skunk cabbage flowers. Wild plum showers its blossoms on the hillside and along the fern-fringed trail.

Red-tailed Hawk.
Photo by Jim Cruce

Directions: From Hwy. 99W, about 3 miles southwest of King City, turn south at the light onto N. Sherwood Boulevard. Travel 0.7 mile, passing two schools on your left. Turn right onto NW 3rd and right again onto NW Washington. Go down the hill and notice that this large grassy park has no sign. Cross Cedar Creek and turn left to find parking.

Amenities:

AREA 9: Lower Tualatin River (West of I-5)

Ibach Park itself is dominated by recreation facilities, including a mile-long paved trail. Common backyard birds abound. With patience, one may hear the loud call of the Killdeer or even spot this plover with its long, reddish tail and two black breast stripes. The far northern end of the park offers access to the Hedges Creek Greenway, a half-mile corridor extending from the creek's headwaters at Ibach Road to 105th Avenue.

Pacific
waterleaf.

Along the greenway the trees include Douglas-fir, red-cedar, and red alder as well as Oregon ash and bigleaf maple. There are small pockets of wetlands on the flatter floodplain, where you can find vine maple, elderberry, rose, willow, snowberry, red-osier dogwood, salal, Oregon-grape, ninebark, and salmonberry. In the early spring, look for the blazing gold spathes of skunk cabbage. Later you will discover wood violets, large false Solomon's seal, twisted-stalk, and Pacific waterleaf. Waterleaf has a small flower and is easily overlooked, although it grows in abundance, often covering a damp forest floor or streamside. Look for its highly divided and slightly hairy leaves. The heads of pale bluish flowers seem hairy, too, since the stamens are much longer than the corollas, or rings of petals.

Birds are plentiful. American Robins, Mourning Doves, Spotted Towhees, Black-capped Chickadees, Steller's Jays, and other backyard birds are in evidence. There are also Downy and Pileated woodpeckers. Raccoons, opossum, and even some deer make their homes here. There are Pacific lamprey and reticulate sculpin as well as salamanders in the creek and, at sunset, the frog chorus is awesome. The creek and its corridor were once engulfed by Himalayan blackberry, but the neighborhood surrounding the park has worked hard with the City of Tualatin Parks Department and local ecologists to remove it, and their efforts have certainly paid off. These efforts are ongoing and the creek and its corridor are ever changing.

Directions: From I-5 take Exit 289 toward Sherwood. Turn left on Boones Ferry Road. Go south for 1.5 miles. Turn right on Ibach Street. The park is 0.4 miles on the right.

Amenities:

5 LITTLE WOOD ROSE NATURE PARK

Trilliums. *Photo by Monte Rumgay*

At one entrance to this park, a sign points out that it is maintained in its natural state by Boy Scout Troop 35, the Tualatin Rotary Club, and the City of Tualatin. That careful maintenance shows in the relative lack of Himalayan blackberry and English ivy, and the consequent health of local species.

Along Boones Ferry Road and ringing the park are mature Douglas-firs and there is an understory of salal, sword fern, and bracken fern. You will also find steeple bush, snowberry, Oregon-grape and, of course, the park's signature plant: wood rose (baldhip rose). Notice its numerous needle-like prickles and the five to nine small leaflets. In summer, it will display tiny, delicate pink flowers.

The trails are fine all-weather gravel, but the terrain is too steep for wheelchair access. Up a small hill, look for young red-cedars and red alders. There is a good variety of deciduous trees; in the fall and early winter look down to enjoy the leaves which litter the ground in a kaleidoscope of sizes, shapes, and colors. Along the path, look for yellow fungus and a surprise patch of spearmint. In the spring you will find showy white trilliums, yellow wood violets, and pink candy flowers.

Expect to see the usual forest birds here (chickadees, nuthatches, wrens, and kinglets) but you may also see a Sharp-shinned Hawk. This small, woodland hawk is about the size of a Western Scrub-Jay with a long, square tail and short, rounded wings. The Sharp-shinned Hawk does not soar as much as, for instance, the Red-tailed Hawk, but instead hops from hedge to hedge using several short wingbeats and a glide.

Directions: From I-5 take Exit 289 toward Sherwood. Turn left on Boones Ferry Road. Turn left on Avery, right on 90th Avenue. Entrance is next to 21075 SW 90th Street.

Amenities:

Vanillaleaf (above).
Trillium (right).
Photos by Susan Peter

Hedges Creek was once a year-round stream but is now only seasonal because of new construction within the basin. Fifty years ago you could catch trout in Hedges Creek. The marsh is two miles long and now bounded almost entirely by industrial and commercial development. In spite of this, the marsh continues to attract a wide variety of wildlife.

There are deer in the area, and occasionally coyote, fox, and river otter can be seen. Beaver and raccoon are abundant in the marsh despite the fact that it is in the middle of Tualatin, a city of 21,000 people.

Many species of ducks enjoy the creek, including Mallards, Wood Ducks, Hooded Mergansers, American Wigeons, Buffleheads, Cinnamon Teal, and Ring-necked Ducks. Canada Geese nest in the marsh and Virginia Rails, Soras, Pied-billed Grebes, and Belted Kingfishers are residents. Songbirds include Red-winged Blackbirds, Common Yellowthroats, and Marsh Wrens. In July, a Killdeer was spied with her three chicks — little round miniatures of the parent. Tree, Violet-green, and Barn swallows patrol the air, as do birds of prey including Barn and Great-horned owls, Red-tailed Hawks, and Northern Harriers. Great Blue Herons are common, and in recent years Great Egrets have been seen. Over 60 species of birds have been listed for this marsh.

Plants and insects also draw one's attention. Fat bumblebees and honeybees buzz over the Canada thistle. Along the fence, steeple bush raises its magenta head. Native black hawthorn is distinguished from the English hawthorn by its slightly lobed oval leaves and purple fruit; English hawthorn has deeply indented leaves and red fruit. Both varieties have creamy white flowers. At any time of year, this is a great place to remind us of what was here before the apartments and the mall.

Directions: From I-5 take Exit 289 toward Sherwood. Just after crossing Boones Ferry Road, turn right into the Hedges Creek Shopping Center. Viewing access is behind the mall. Look for a wooden pedestrian bridge. You can also view from the Tualatin Post Office parking lot and where Teton Road crosses the marsh a mile farther west of Boones Ferry Road.

Black hawthorn (top).
English hawthorn (bottom).

Amenities:

What's The Goop?
Bryozoa in the Tualatin River

By Bob Paulson

Y ou may have seen it, an irregular fuzzy-looking, grayish-brown gob of goop wrapped around a submerged tree limb, ranging in size from a dot on a leaf to larger than a basketball.

If you have, feel lucky, for few people notice this aquatic prize at all. Although opinions vary that the mass is someone's lost brain, fish eggs, strange moss, pollution sludge, or an oversized freshwater sponge, it is none of these. Each round gelatinous mass is an intricate colony of thousands of essentially inseparable individual animal beings called "zooids," collectively called Bryozoa or moss animals. The individual organisms are nearly microscopic and join together like twigs of an intertwined bush to produce what looks from the outside like a solid homogenous unit. About 3,500 species of marine Bryozoans exist worldwide, of which 15 of the 50 freshwater species can be found in North America.

When Bryozoa are viewed under a 40-power microscope, one sees each member of the colony has a halo of ciliated tentacles surrounding its mouth. Tentacles capture algae, protozoa, and miniscule debris upon which Bryozoa feed. The colonies generally do not move, but some of the freshwater species can sluggishly creep. So far, Bryozoa haven't been shown to be an important part of the food chain of other animals. However, they can clog screens of industrial or agricultural water intakes.

Bryozoa attach themselves to the underside of submerged rocks, logs, and tree limbs, since they prefer dim light. However, most I have seen on the Tualatin River were obvious under the water's surface and wrapped around the limbs of submerged dead trees.

Don't worry if you've touched one; these animals are harmless. I discovered several clumps between river mile 17 and the Schamburg Bridge (river mile 16.2). Finding Bryozoa in the Tualatin River is a good sign because they occur only in unpolluted and unsilted waters, particularly in ponds, shallow portions of lakes, and slow-moving quiet streams. They are found in some stagnant waters, but not in polluted water, and only sparingly where the level of dissolved oxygen falls below 30 percent saturation. They are most commonly seen in the Tualatin at the end of summer.

So next time you're on the Tualatin River, look for Bryozoa. You may find your search as intriguing as birdwatching.

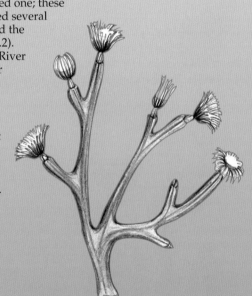

Bryozoa as seen magnified 40x.
Drawing by Barbara Macomber

This Wetlands Conservancy property is on Apache Bluff adjacent to the Tualatin Country Club. An undeveloped wildlife preserve, it is separated from the Tualatin River by the golf course. The preserve holds water all winter, but becomes partially or totally dry in the summer months.

Waterfowl that frequent Apache Bluff include Canada Geese, Mallards, Wood Ducks, Hooded Mergansers, Buffleheads, and American Wigeons. Birdwatchers have also sighted Great Blue Herons, Green Herons, American Bitterns, Common Snipes, Killdeer, Bewick's Wrens, Red-winged Blackbirds, and several species of swallows. The wetland also has some dense brush and there are deer, raccoon, and beaver.

In the grasses at the edge of the preserve you may notice three introduced flowers: the pretty rosita, or European centaury, with its sweet pink trumpets and minute, spirally twisted anthers; Queen Anne's lace (wild carrot) with its flat heads of numerous tiny white flowers; and self-heal, a member of the Mint Family. Self-heal was an early introduction to North America and has long been used to heal cuts, bruises, and skin inflammations. This flower's Latin name, *Prunella*, is derived from the German for quinsy, a throat inflammation, for which this plant was considered a cure.

Directions: From I-5 take Exit 289 toward Sherwood. Turn north onto Boones Ferry Road. Stay in the left lane to continue north. The road veers left becoming Tualatin Road. Turn right onto Cheyenne Way (immediately west of the Tualatin Country Club and a few feet east of the Herman Road junction). Cheyenne Way ends at a barricade. Two paths lead away from here. The more obvious one leads, not to the preserve, but through an open area to the fringes of the golf course. The other, a shady lane to the right of the barricade, follows the property line of 17370 SW Cheyenne Way. Follow this lane down the hill to the pond. Although this is private property, The Wetland Conservancy happily welcomes responsible visitors. From here, a mowed pathway to the left leads to other viewing areas.

Amenities:

Killdeer
with chick.
Photo by Jim Cruce

AREA 9: Lower Tualatin River (West of I-5)

8 COOK PARK

As you go down the hill into Cook Park, notice the mitigation wetlands on both sides of the street. Those to the west are good for viewing wading birds such as herons and an occasional Great Egret. On the east side of the road, the cat-tail marsh is favored by Red-winged Blackbirds, Belted Kingfishers, Barn Swallows, and Violet-green Swallows. Winter brings a variety of waterfowl to these wetlands, including Buffleheads, Hooded Mergansers, and Green-winged Teals.

Roses, rhododendrons, picnic shelters, and lawns make this city park a summertime favorite, but native flora also abounds. Follow the trails through riparian woodlands where there are Pacific yew trees. In the undergrowth, native thimbleberries and salmonberries vie with introduced Himalayan blackberries. During the summer months, you will see the distinctive wild cucumber vines. Also called "old-man-in-the-ground" because of its huge root, this plant has large, palmately lobed leaves, small white flowers, curling tendrils, and two-inch football-shaped fruits. Watch out for stinging nettles; if you touch the hairy leaves, the hairs break and release formic acid, which causes a painful rash. Nevertheless, nettles were important to the Atfalati. They cooked and ate the young shoots, but more important, the nettles were their source of fiber for making fishnets, snares, and tump-lines.

This is a good place to see red elderberry. In contrast to the blue elder-berry's flat top clusters of fragrant white flowers and edible blue fruits, the red elderberry's flowers appear in a rounded or pyramidal cluster and have an unpleasant smell. Its fruits are bright red and the Native Americans knew they must always be cooked or they would cause nausea. The stems, bark, leaves, and roots are toxic due to the presence of cyanide-producing glycocides.

Look for a variety of woodland birds. Wood-boring birds such as Pileated Woodpeckers, Northern Flickers, and Downy Woodpeckers can be seen (and heard) as they seek food in the wood bark.

Directions: Going south on Hwy. 99W, in King City, turn left (east) onto Durham Road. Just before Tigard High School, turn right onto 92nd at the sign.

Amenities:

Red elderberry.
Photo by Susan Peter

9 TUALATIN COMMUNITY PARK

Chestnut-backed Chickadee.
Photo by Michael Wilhelm

This city park borders the Tualatin River, although river access is limited to the boat ramp. Walking north underneath the railway trestle, you quickly leave the hustle of the busy park and enter the quiet groves of Douglas-fir and bigleaf maples. Here, the soft notes of Chestnut-backed Chickadees and the tin trumpet fanfare of Brown Creepers are offset by the raucous chatter of Belted Kingfishers from over the river.

Look under the canopy of trees for the arching stems of the large false Solomon's seal. The plumes of tiny flowers are creamy white and later will give way to speckled round red poisonous berries. The name marks the plant's resemblance to Solomon's seal (a native of the Eastern U. S.), which gets its name from the six-pointed star markings on its root. Look also for duckfoot leaves; the name is quite descriptive, as is its other name, inside-out-flower, which describes the tiny creamy white flowers, several on each stem, which turn themselves inside-out, the stamens and pistils hanging below the petals. There are also snowberry, salal, and sword fern (turn one over to see the spores which produce the next generation of plants). In spring the trillium flaunts its three white petals over a whorl of three leaves. Gradually the flowers turn pink to purple and by summer only the leaves remain.

Sadly, the wildflower treasures of the park are being smothered by the invasive English ivy that covers the ground and climbs high into the trees. Clearly, community action is called for before much of this beautiful area succumbs to the invader.

Directions: From I-5 take Exit 289 toward Sherwood. Turn right at Boones Ferry Road. Spot the low railroad trestle ahead and go straight (north) toward it. Drive under the trestle to find a parking lot near the woodsy area described above.

Amenities:

Paddling the Tualatin.
Photo by Michael Wilhelm

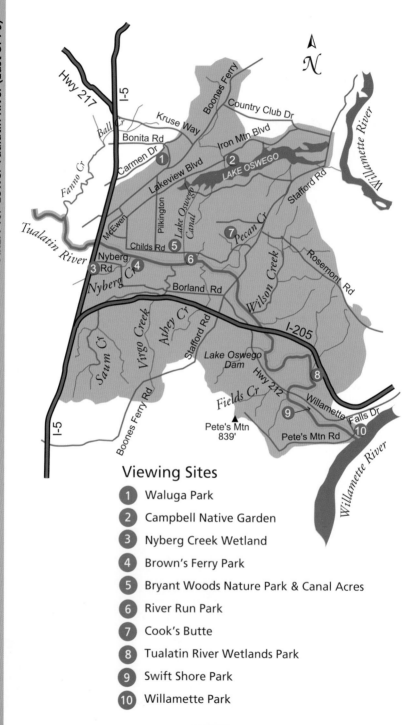

Viewing Sites

1 Waluga Park

2 Campbell Native Garden

3 Nyberg Creek Wetland

4 Brown's Ferry Park

5 Bryant Woods Nature Park & Canal Acres

6 River Run Park

7 Cook's Butte

8 Tualatin River Wetlands Park

9 Swift Shore Park

10 Willamette Park

VIEWING AREA 10: Lower Tualatin River (East of I-5)

The Tualatin River flows 30 river miles between Rood Bridge in Hillsboro (river mile 38.44) and Boone's Bridge at I-5 (river mile 8.18). The convoluted bends and oxbow lakes that are the Tualatin's loopy signature exist here because, lacking a steep grade, the flow tends to puddle and wander. In fact, it loses less than 10 feet of elevation between these bridges.

The meanders are left behind, though, as the river passes through the City of Tualatin. From here, as if spilling from an overflowing bowl, the river descends rapidly, losing more than 50 feet of elevation in only eight miles. Because of this increased gradient, the channel becomes straighter and more purposeful.

The canal that diverts the Tualatin's water to Lake Oswego is found at river mile 6.70. This canal passes through a low region between Bull Mountain and Cook's Butte. Some geologists believe this low passage marks one of the Tualatin's prehistoric channels. It is unusual for a river to have an increased gradient near its outlet; it often marks a geologic shift, and this prehistoric channel fits that scenario. A dam on the Tualatin at river mile 3.45 keeps water levels high enough to assure summer flow through the canal to Lake Oswego.

The lower Tualatin's rapid elevation loss is not apparent above the dam. However, below the dam, all the way to the Willamette (river mile 0.0), white water is frequently visible. In-flowing streams below the canal are short and steep. This is further evidence of a comparatively recent change in the river's channel.

At its mouth, our valley is narrowed into a chute between Rosemont Ridge to the north and Pete's Mountain to the south. Rosemont Ridge is an extension of Cook's Butte and is the hill on which West Linn is built. Pete's Mountain is a mass of rock; the edge of it forms the rather formidable basalt cliff seen across the river from Swift Shore Park. The Tualatin, widely known for its cool green stillness, manages to make a rather splashy ending in its final miles.

Willamette Park in West Linn (see page 150). *Photo by Brian Wegener*

Waluga Drive splits these two Waluga Parks and clearly defines the limits of each. Most of West Waluga is a typical city park with a covered picnic area, play equipment, and a mowed lawn with an asphalt path. The plantings feature Pacific Northwest flowers and trees such as red-osier dogwood. Note the red branches, clusters of small white flowers (quite unlike the large flowers of the common dogwood), and white berries. There are several varieties of wild rose, and some steeple bush (hardhack).

Waluga, to the east, is the "wild park." There is a wide, packed gravel path bordered on its north by Douglas-fir and Oregon white oak. Watch out for poison oak near the beginning of this trail. English ivy, a scourge of many western Oregon parks, has also gained ground by climbing up trees. This ivy will eventually choke and kill the trees. Near the end of the trail you will see some Scotch broom, whose golden flowers vie with the yellow of the great mullein; both are of European introduction.

On the south side of the trail are service berry bushes, many of which are covered with gray-green lichens. The service berry is one of many bushes with small white flowers. It has a unique and memorable little leaf, however. Look for almost-round leaves about one inch across, that have smooth round margins on the stem half and serrations on the tip half. Beyond these, closer to the water, are reed canarygrass, buttercup, and knotweed.

Together, both of the Waluga parks offer a wide variety of bird habitats in a very small space. The perimeter of West Waluga Park has wetlands with large snags. Look for woodpeckers here and in the Oregon white oaks on higher ground. Waluga Park's forested wetlands are a good place to look for song-birds. Listen for the repetitious song of the Black-capped Chickadee. The blackberry thickets in the Douglas-fir on the hill hide Song Sparrows and Dark-eyed Juncos. Look up. Sharp-shinned Hawks fly overhead looking for a meal of small birds and small mammals. And did you know that Waluga was the original Native American name for Lake Oswego? It means "wild swan."

Directions: Take I-5 Exit 291. Go east on Carmen Drive. Turn right on Waluga Drive.

Amenities:

Dark-eyed Junco.
Photo by Monte Rumgay

CAMPBELL NATIVE GARDEN

This is a tiny garden on a fraction of an acre. While the trees above Springbrook Creek are filled with bird song and the benches are new and well placed, the garden is also special for other reasons: the labeled native plants and the creek's unique relationship to the Tualatin River.

A soft trail of crushed filbert (hazelnut) shells winds through this garden where some two dozen natives have been planted and labeled with common and scientific names. Among others, find wild ginger, evergreen huckleberry, Pacific bleeding-heart, and red-flowering currant.

This creek flows into Lake Oswego, but also has a sign indicating it is part of the Tualatin River watershed. While this seems contradictory, since Lake Oswego drains directly to the Willamette, it is also true that the Tualatin River and Lake Oswego are connected by a canal. Therefore, Lake Oswego is a passageway by which Tualatin River waters exit the Tualatin Basin. Geologic evidence suggests that the Tualatin's main channel once joined the Willamette by flowing through the route now occupied by the canal and Lake Oswego.

Directions: From I-5 take Exit 290. Take Lower Boones Ferry Road toward Lake Oswego; just past Pilkington turn right onto SW Upper Drive. After almost 2 miles on Upper Drive, cross Twin Fir Road and go down the hill and through a traffic circle at the intersection with Lakeview Boulevard. The park is on the right at the base of the hill. A gravel shoulder provides parking for about two cars (the Lake Oswego Hunt Club is across the street). Upper Drive becomes Iron Mountain Boulevard here, and a bike path continues from here into downtown Lake Oswego.

Amenities: 🅿

Bleeding-heart (above).

Wild ginger (left).
Photos by Susan Peter

AREA 10: Lower Tualatin River (East of I-5)

3 | NYBERG CREEK WETLAND

This wetland was once a reed canarygrass monoculture, but excavation has created open water ponds adjacent to Nyberg Creek. Fish that swim up the creek from the Tualatin River provide food for herons, fish-eating ducks, kingfishers, and an occasional Osprey. Canada Geese and Mallards are common and, in spring, watch for baby ducks and geese. Beavers are also common.

Around the parking lot and into the wetland, wildflowers flourish. The pretty pink flowers of the wild rose later produce red hips; these are rich in Vitamin C. The magenta pink spikes of steeple bush are also in bloom throughout the summer. The Latin name for this plant, *Spiraea douglasii*, reminds us that this plant is one of 150 collected by Scottish botanist David Douglas (1798-1834) and taken to Britain from the Pacific Northwest.

Directions: From I-5 take Exit 289. Go east on Nyberg Road only a few hundred feet. Turn right at the gas station/convenience store and park at the strip mall. Viewing is from the balcony under the "7000 Nyberg" sign or inside El Sol de Mexico Restaurant.

Amenities:

Pied-billed Grebe.
Photo by Jim Cruce

Some Like it Wet

Great Blue Heron.
Jim Cruce

Corn lily. *Susan Peter*

Blue darner (dragonfly).
Steve Berliner

Marsh Wren (far right).
Bittern (below).
Michael Wilhelm

Veronica. *Susan Peter*

4 BROWN'S FERRY PARK

Pearly everlasting.
Photo by Susan Peter

Brown's Ferry Park from 1850 to 1856 was the site of a ferry set up by one Zenas Brown, described as "an eclectic physician." Later, the land was farmed and an old barn still remains.

To the west, closest to the park entrance and parking lot, is Nyberg Creek. This small stream has a resident beaver population and well-established riparian edge of large ash trees. Within minutes you may hear the rattling cry of a Belted Kingfisher. Beneath the Oregon ash, bigleaf maples, and black hawthorns is a jungle of undergrowth. Look close to the stream for a pretty little yellow and red-orange flower with three fused petals, the upper one ending in a long spur. This is jewelweed, or more descriptively, touch-me-not, because the ripe fruits burst open when touched.

The confluence of Nyberg Creek and the Tualatin River has a marker to show the height of the Tualatin during the floods of 1996. There is a bench overlooking the cool, green river where you can enjoy the Monet-like reflection of trees in water. If you are lucky, an Osprey may be seen flying up or down the river. Watch, too, for the ubiquitous nutria. On the land side of the trail is a naturalized meadow planted to native northwest wildflowers. In the fall, only a few California poppies, some pearly everlasting, and non-native Queen Anne's lace survive the summer, but earlier in the year this is a symphony of color.

Following the river, the trail crosses another small stream. Here you can head away from the Tualatin towards Nyberg Road, circling a small wetland complete with Mallards, Wood Ducks, Buffleheads, Wigeons, and other ducks. This area supports a variety of wetland plants as well as a population of noisy bullfrogs. A viewing blind has been built by the Tualatin Parks Department. An alternate trail follows the Tualatin to the park boundary.

Watch for bracken and sword fern in the undergrowth, English holly and hazel bushes, and some red-cedars and red alders in the canopy. At the river's edge, a big patch of pretty purple Douglas' asters catches the eye. In England, where this flower is an introduced garden favorite, it is known as "Michaelmas daisy" because it flowers around the Feast of St. Michael, September 29th.

6 RIVER RUN PARK

Common Yellowthroat. *Photo by Jim Cruce*

Except for the gravel path leading to the river, this is an undeveloped park. The Lake Oswego Canal is to the right; you might want to stop to admire the new control gate structures, rebuilt after the 1996 flood.

The bank of the Tualatin is high and steep at the canal inlet, but if you follow the small trail between the meadow and the trees you'll find the bank becomes lower. This trail only runs a few hundred yards, but the thick brush and trees in a narrow band along the river provide good riparian habitat for birds. Some very large Oregon ash shade a snowberry thicket; buttercups, fringe-cups, and ferns grow under it. Along the river, listen for the rattle call of the Belted Kingfisher.

Song Sparrows are common in the open areas, and in the summer, look carefully for the Common Yellowthroat, a beautiful yellow warbler with a black mask. They are more often heard than seen; their "wichety-wichety" call is distinctive. In the grassy meadow there are some common wildflowers: chicory blazes bright blue and Queen Anne's lace still blooms well into fall. A few large old apple trees are beautiful with their pink blossoms in the spring and are a reminder of the changes that have occurred along the river.

This river was once the best highway available. Mills were built along it, many ferries crossed it, and amusement parks for swimming, picnicking, and dancing lined its banks until the 1950s when pollution made the river unsuitable for swimming. This site, right next to the canal entrance, has probably seen several different uses.

The canal, dug by Chinese laborers, was completed in the fall of 1872. It supposedly saw its first commercial traffic on January 21, 1873 when Captain Joseph Kellog's barge, the *Onward*, carried 2,000 bushels of wheat to market. This story is in dispute, as the barge would have been too wide for the narrow canal. Its success as a commercial waterway was short lived — a railroad was soon built from Portland along the north shore of Lake Oswego and into the Tualatin Valley.

Directions: From I-5 take Exit 290. Go east on Lower Boones Ferry Road towards Lake Oswego. Turn right on Pilkington Road. Left on SW Childs Road. Right on River Run Drive to a cul-de-sac at its end. There is no sign.

Amenities:

AREA 10: Lower Tualatin River (East of I-5)

145

Common Ferns of the Tualatin River Basin
By Susan Peter

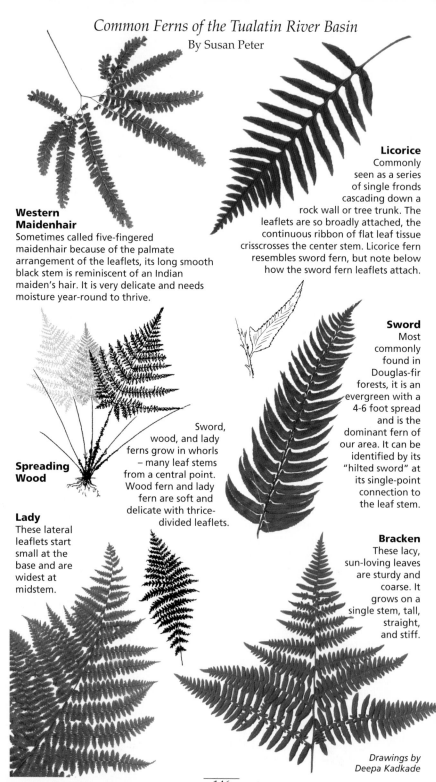

Licorice
Commonly seen as a series of single fronds cascading down a rock wall or tree trunk. The leaflets are so broadly attached, the continuous ribbon of flat leaf tissue crisscrosses the center stem. Licorice fern resembles sword fern, but note below how the sword fern leaflets attach.

Western Maidenhair
Sometimes called five-fingered maidenhair because of the palmate arrangement of the leaflets, its long smooth black stem is reminiscent of an Indian maiden's hair. It is very delicate and needs moisture year-round to thrive.

Sword
Most commonly found in Douglas-fir forests, it is an evergreen with a 4-6 foot spread and is the dominant fern of our area. It can be identified by its "hilted sword" at its single-point connection to the leaf stem.

Spreading Wood

Sword, wood, and lady ferns grow in whorls – many leaf stems from a central point. Wood fern and lady fern are soft and delicate with thrice-divided leaflets.

Lady
These lateral leaflets start small at the base and are widest at midstem.

Bracken
These lacy, sun-loving leaves are sturdy and coarse. It grows on a single stem, tall, straight, and stiff.

Drawings by Deepa Kadkade

7 COOK'S BUTTE

Salal.
Photo by Susan Peter

Cook's Butte offers an upland forest and the promise of a view over the lower Tualatin Valley. The native plants in the understory are typical of forests throughout the area: salal, Oregon-grape, thimbleberry, sword fern, and hazel. Salal and Oregon-grape are both evergreen with shiny hard leaves, usually only knee-high — except at the coast. Salal has drooping racemes of 3/8 inch white lantern-shaped flowers, and almost black fruits. Oregon-grape has a prickly leaf reminiscent of holly. Its thick spikes of bright yellow flowers are hard to miss. Fruit is a cluster of round blue berries. Fruits from both plants are edible, but rarely considered tasty.

To find a view amongst all these trees is not easy. After climbing the trail to a partially hidden water tower, turn left to get to a meadow with a bit of a view to the southeast. Or instead, stay on the wide main pathway down the hill about 100 yards. Turn right where boulders block a grassy side road. This road ends on the top of a second water tank where, in the past, one could obtain spectacular views to the south and west. When there are no leaves on the trees, you can spot (to the right) a bit of the west end of Lake Oswego and, behind it, the spires of the Latter-day Saints Temple by the I-5/Highway 217 interchange. Left of that are the eastern slopes of Bull Mountain, rapidly being denuded for housing. Looking farther to the left (toward the southwest), the Tualatin River is tucked out of sight behind the low wooded ridge in the foreground.

You can expect to see the usual forest birds including Steller's Jays, nuthatches, and chickadees. Sometimes, at migration times, the higher hills such as Cook's Butte will host an assortment of songbirds. These are hard to identify, so bring your bird book. Also, be sure to look up. You may get a close-up view of migrating flocks of geese or even Sandhill Cranes.

Directions: From I-205, take Exit 3, and go north on Stafford Road. Left on Overlook (near Lakeridge High School.) Left on Hillside Drive. Left on Palisades Crest Drive. Drive to the end of the road. Walk in past the gate.

Amenities:

Sandhill Crane. *Photo by Jim Cruce*

AREA 10: Lower Tualatin River (East of I-5)

8 | TUALATIN RIVER WETLANDS PARK

The Tualatin River Wetlands Park is a restoration project designed to return this seven-acre site to a healthy floodplain. Thanks to help from the Willamette Primary School and Envirocorps, today native plants replace blackberry tangles. Sword fern, skunk cabbage, and Oregon-grape flourish under the shade of bigleaf maples and Pacific willows. The wildlife appreciate the change. In the spring, the Red-winged Blackbirds can be heard staking out their territory. The presence of Pileated Woodpeckers is signaled by the "rat-tat-tat" of beaks against wood as they chisel trees in search of insects. Pileated Woodpeckers, common in Oregon, are big and black with a red crest. In flight, their underwing areas flash white. Mallards and Canada Geese are also common, as are Belted Kingfishers. Great Blue Heron fish the waters. In the meadow, Pacific chorus frogs and garter snakes thrive.

A long gravel trail leads down the steep slope to the floodplain of the quietly flowing river . The riverbanks are lined with steeple bush, bigleaf maples, and red-cedars.

Directions: From I-205 take Exit 6. Go south on 10th Street. Right on Willamette Falls Drive. Right on Dollar Street. Right on Ostman Road to Michael Court. Entrance is between 2430 and 2410 Michael Court.

Amenities:

Elbow Bend at Swift Shore Park.
Photo by Susan Peter

9 SWIFT SHORE PARK

Do you consider the Tualatin River a slow-flowing, green, meandering waterway — lovely in its own way, but not to be compared with swifter, more lively streams? Then you must visit the aptly named Swift Shore Park to see the Tualatin in a different mood.

The Swift Shore Drive neighbors of this little treasure of a park are quick to tell you about the wildlife, including

Red-winged Blackbird.
Photo by Jim Cruce

Bald Eagles, Great Blue Herons, and Ospreys. The duck population includes Mallards and Wood Ducks. Canada Geese are common. Hummingbirds flit among the residents' flowers. People who have bird feeders recognize House Finches, Steller's Jays, Western Scrub-Jays, and Black-capped Chickadees. Northern Flickers are common and at least two pairs of Belted Kingfishers nest nearby. Squirrels play in the trees; there are raccoons and an occasional deer.

Access 1: To reach the river, take the path between two houses and cross the grass. Watch out for poison oak. Listen. Hear the sound of swift water. See how the deep green Tualatin speeds over the big boulders in the riverbed. The opposite shore is a high, steep bank, wild and still forested. You may wish to follow the public trail along the river to the right.

Access 2: Now, go a few houses down the road to the foot of Swift Shore Circle. Follow the path between the houses and out to a lawn. Nearby our swift river has turned frivolous as white water rushes over the rocks, only to catch its breath as it forms a cool, deep pool at Elbow Bend. Neighbors say this is their swimming hole. There is even a rope swing over the water.

Listen to the sounds of the rushing water and the occasional loud, high rattle of a Belted Kingfisher. There are more cascades to the east of Elbow Bend, but no access; the trail leads only west. Oregon ash trees, tilted or uprooted by past floods, are decorated with vines: morning glory, wild clematis, and bittersweet nightshade. There are baldhip (wood) roses, a snowberry or two, a little knotweed, and some salal. But these are simply the supporting acts. In Swift Shore Park the Tualatin is the star of the show.

Directions: From I-205 take Exit 6. Turn south onto 10th Street.
Right on Willamette Falls Drive. Left on Swift Shore Drive.
Access 1: Between 25375 and 25345 Swift Shore Drive.
Access 2: Between 25455 and 25465 Swift Shore Circle.

Amenities:

149

10 WILLAMETTE PARK

Willamette Park in West Linn is at the confluence of the Tualatin River and the mighty Willamette. There is something for everyone here, even folks looking for wildlife. The Tualatin is on your right as you enter the park on 12th Street. After you park, look in this direction to find a small beach and The Tualatin Riverkeepers' sign designating this as river mile 0.0 of the Tualatin. Some people consider this little beach to be the best part of the park. Look here for Spotted Sandpipers with their characteristic bobbing and teetering. Spotted Sandpipers are one of a few polyandrous birds — a female may mate with several males. A female may lay up to five clutches of eggs, one to four eggs in each clutch. The care of the eggs and chicks is performed by the males, each male caring for one clutch.

Above the beach, a grove of Oregon ash and Douglas-fir shelters an understory of wild roses and snowberries. Along the river's edge you will see tall black cottonwood trees. This stretch of the Tualatin is where you are likely to see western Oregon's three most common herons: Great Blue Heron, Green Heron, and Great Egret.

If you walk up the hill you can get a great view of the river from Weiss Bridge. Looking upstream, the Tualatin shows the same rocky riffle characteristics as it does in its headwaters. In summer, the bridge is a great place to get a bird's-eye view of acrobatic flights of Violet-green and Barn swallows as they catch insects on the wing. In the fall and winter, look downstream from the bridge for a variety of waterfowl including Canada Geese, Mallards, and mergansers.

Directions: From I-205 take Exit 6. Turn south onto 10th Street. Turn right on Willamette Falls Drive. Left on 12th Street. At the stop sign remain on 12th and go straight down the hill.

Amenities:

Great Egret.
*Photo by
Jim Cruce*

BIBLIOGRAPHY

Beckham, Stephen Dow. *The Indians of Western Oregon: This Land Was Theirs.* Orago Books, Coos Bay, OR, 1977

Coming, Howard McKinley. *Willamette Landings.* Oregon Historical Society, Portland, OR, 1973

Cooke, Sarah Spear, editor. *A Field Guide to the Common Wetland Plants of Western Washington and Northwestern Oregon.* Seattle Audubon Society, Seattle, WA, 1997

Engstrom, W.H. *Flowering Shrubs Native to Western Oregon.* Oregon State Forestry Department, Salem, OR, 1971

Gilkey, Helen M., and La Rea J. Dennis. *Handbook of Northwestern Plants.* Oregon State University Press, Corvallis, OR, 2001

Guard, B. Jennifer. *Wetland Plants of Oregon and Washington.* Lone Pine Publishing, Redmond, WA, 1995

Haskin, Leslie L. *Wildflowers of the Pacific Coast.* Metropolitan Press, Portland, OR, 1934

Kirk, Donald R. *Wild Edible Plants of Western North America.* Naturegraph Publishers, Inc., Happy Camp, CA, 1975

Mackey, Harold. *The Kalapuyans: A Sourcebook on the Indians of the Willamette Valley.* Mission Mill Museum Association, Salem, OR, 1974

McMinn, Howard E., and Evelyn Maino. *An Illustrated Manual of Pacific Coast Trees.* University of California Press, Berkeley, CA, 1946

Martin, Alexander C. *Weeds.* Golden Press, New York, NY, 1987

Martinazzi, Loyce, and Karen Lafky Nygaard. *Tualatin From the Beginning.* Tualatin Historical Society, Tualatin, OR, 1974

Moore, Virginia, editor. *Land of the Tualaty.* Washington County Historical Society, Hillsboro, OR, 1976

Nehls, Harry B. *Familiar Birds of the Northwest.* Audubon Society of Portland, Portland, OR 1989

Niehaus, Theodore F., and Charles L. Ripper. *A Field Guide to Pacific States Wildflowers.* Houghton Mifflin Co, Boston, MA, 1976

Peter, Susan. *A Small, Totally Incomplete Guide to Plant Identification for the Pacific Northwest.* Beaverton, OR, 1998

Peterson, Roger Tory. *A Field Guide to Western Birds.* Houghton Mifflin Co., Boston, MA, 1961

Pojar, Jim, and Andy MacKinnon, editors. *Plants of the Pacific Northwest Coast.* Lone Pine Publishing, Redmond, WA, 1994

Robbins, Chandler S., Bertel Bruun, and Herbert S. Zim. *Birds of North American.* Golden Press, New York, NY, 1966

Spellenberg, Richard. *The Audubon Society Field Guide to North American Wildflowers: Western Region.* Alfred A. Knopf, New York, NY. 1979

Sunset Magazine. *Western Garden Book.* Lane Magazine and Book Co., Menlo Park, CA, 1977

Watts, Tom. *Pacific Coast Tree Finder.* Nature Study Guild, Berkeley, CA, 1973

Whittlesey, Rhoda. *Familiar Friends: Northwest Plants.* Rose Press, Portland, OR, 1985

Wilson, Kim. *Common Street Trees of Portland.* Saturday Academy Program of Oregon Graduate Institute of Science and Technology, Beaverton, OR, 2000

Tualatin Watershed Friends Groups

For additional information and contacts,
visit www.tualatinriverkeepers.org, or call (503) 590-5813.

Bridlemile Creek Stewards
(503) 768-9065, (503) 246-2714
steve.mullinax@worldnet.att.net
gregsch@hevanet.com

Cedar Mill Creek Watershed Watch
(503) 288-9338
gvadnais@spiretech.com

Crestwood Headwaters Group
(503) 925-9703 (work)

Fans of Fanno Creek
(503) 916-5690
info@fansoffannocreek.org
www.fansoffannocreek.org

Friends of Beaverton Creek
503) 224-1064
bonnieisbirding@prodigy.net

Friends of Beaverton's Johnson Creek
(503) 579-1161
fbjc@safe-mail.net

Friends of Bryant Woods
(503) 638-7991

Friends of Butternut Creek
(503) 591-7850
dpmarvin@easystreet.com

Friends of Cook Park
(503) 639-5039

Friends of Fernhill Wetlands
(503) 357-5890
brattae@pdx.edu

Friends of Golf Creek
(503) 292-4549, fax: (503) 297-7907

Friends of Rock, Bronson &
Willow Creeks
(503) 629-8862
hilll@pacifier.com

Friends of the Tualatin River
National Wildlife Refuge
(503) 972-7714
chateaul@teleport.com

Skyline Ridge Neighbors Natural
Resources Committee
(503) 621-3552
gsowder@teleport.com

Double-crested Cormorant.
Photo by Jim Cruce

Index

Bold = Picture; *Italics* = Description

Bold = Picture; *Italics* = Description

Bold = Picture; *Italics* = Description

Pheasant, Ring-necked, 12
Philadelphus lewisii. See Mock orange
Physocarpus capitatus. See Ninebark
Picea pungens. See Spruce, blue
Picea sitchensis. See Spruce, Sitka
Pigeon, Band-tailed, 104
Piggy-back plant (*Tolmiea menziesii*), *10*
Pimpernel, Scarlet (*Anagallis arvensis*).
   See Scarlet Pimpernel
Pine
   lodgepole (*Pinus contorta*, coast), *16*, 111
   ponderosa (*Pinus ponderosa*), *114*
Plantain
   broad-leaved (*Plantago major*), **72**, *83*
   English (*Plantago lanceolata*, black
     plantain), **72**, *83*
Plantain, rattlesnake (*Goodyera
   oblongifolia*). See Rattlesnake plantain
Plum, wild. See Indian plum (*Oemleria
   cerasiformis*)
Poison hemlock (*Conium maculatum*), *20*
Poison oak (*Toxicodendron diversilobum*),
   6, **30**, 80, *84*, 123, 136
Polygonum aviculare. See Knotweed
Polygonum hydropiperoides.
   See Waterpepper
Polypodium glycyrrhiza. See Fern, licorice
Polystichum munitum. See Fern, sword
Pond-lily, western yellow (*Nuphar
   polysepalum*), **25**, *29*
Poppy, California (*Eschscholzia
   californica*), **113**, 140
Populus trichoscarpa. See Cottonwood
Possum. See Opossum
Potentilla gracilis. See Five-finger
Prairie scouring rush (*Equisetum
   hyemale*), *141*
Praying mantis, **28**, 123
Primrose, evening (*Oenothera biennis*).
   See Evening primrose
Prosartes smithii. See Fairy lanterns
Prunella vulgaris. See Self-heal
Prunus spp. See Cherry
Pseudotsuga menziesii. See Douglas-fir
Pteridium aquilinum. See Fern, bracken

Q
Quail, California, 7
Queen Anne's lace (*Daucus carota*, wild
   carrot), **12**, 56, *131*, 140, 145
Queen's cup (*Clintonia uniflora*, bead
   lily), 9
Quercus garryana. See Oak, Oregon white

R
Rabbit, 22, **34,** 62, 142
Raccoon, 16, 22, **38**, **47**, 55, 62, 98, 129, 131
Rail, Virginia, *15*, 104, 129
Raleighwood Park, 100
Ranunculus uncinatus. See Buttercup
Rattlesnake plantain (*Goodyera
   oblongifolia*), *9*
Raven, Common, *14*, 70, 109, 114
Red-cedar, western (*Thuja plicata*), 16,
   22, **33**, 52, 53, 56, 67, 98, 99, *110*, **144**
Rhamnus purshiana. See Cascara
Rhubarb, Indian (*Darmera peltata*).
   See Indian rhubarb
Ribes sanguineum.
   See Currant, red-flowering
Rippling Waters Nature Park, 10
River Run Park, 145
Robin, American, 10, 40, **41**, 56, 109, 126
Robinia pseudoacacia. See Locust, black
Rock Creek Nature Preserve, 26
Rodgers Park, 11
Rood Bridge Road Park, *43*, 77
Rorippa nasturtium-aquaticum.
   See Water-cress
Rosa gymnocarpa. See Rose, baldhip
Rosa nutkana. See Rose, common wild
Rosa Park, 96
Rosa pisocarpa. See Rose, clustered wild
Rosa rugosa, 70
Rose, 123, 136, **143**
   baldhip (*Rosa gymnocarpa*, little wood
     rose), 8, 62, *101*, *128*, 149
   clustered wild (*Rosa pisocarpa*), 62
   common wild (*Rosa nutkana*), 29, 80,
     109, *138*
Rosita (*Centaurium* spp., centaury*)*, 56,
   72, *131*
Rubus laciniatus. See Blackberry,
   evergreen
Rubus parviflorus. See Thimbleberry
Rubus armeniacus. See Blackberry,
   Himalayan
Rubus spectabilis. See Salmonberry
Rubus ursinus. See Blackberry, trailing
Rudbeckia hirta. See Black-eyed Susan
Rumex acetosella. See Dock, sour
Rumex crispus. See Dock, curly
Rush (*Juncaceae*), 40, *48*, *49*, 70,
   80, 85, 96
   daggerleaf (*Juncus ensifolius*), 60
   scouring (*Equisetum hyemale*).
     See Prairie scouring rush
   soft (*Juncus effusus*, common), 62, 65

Bold = Picture; *Italics* = Description

S

Sagittaria latifolia. See Wapato
St. John's wort (*Hypericum perforatum*), 6, *122*, **124**
Salal (*Gaultheria shallon*), 6, 9, 62, 83, 85, 127, 133, **147**
Salamander, 55, **91**, 127, 142
Salix babylonica. See Willow, weeping
Salix discolor. See Willow, pussy
*Salix matsudana tortuos*a. See Willow, corkscrew
Salix spp. See Willow, native
Salix Park, 65
Salmon, 22, 73
    See also Trout
Salmonberry (*Rubus spectabilis*), 67, 127, 132
Sambucus mexicana. See Elderberry, blue
Sambucus racemosa. See Elderberry, red
Sandpiper,
    Spotted, **48**, *150*
    Western, 48
Scarlet Pimpernel (*Anagallis arvensis*), 27
Scholls Business Center Wetland, 112
Scirpus microcarpus.
    See Bulrush, small-fruited
Scirpus validus. See Bulrush, softstem
Scotch broom (*Cytisus scoparius*), 6, 14, 101, 113, 123, *136*
Scrophularia californica.
    See Figwort, California
Sculpin, 29, 61, 62, 65, 94, 127
Sedge (*Carex* spp.), 12, 40, *48*, *49*, 96, 104
    awl-fruited (*Carex stipata*), 60
Self-heal (*Prunella vulgaris*), 43, 56, *117*, *131*
Sequoia, giant (*Sequoiadendron giganteum*), 16, 47
Service berry (*Amelancier alnifolia*), **35**, 62, **63**, 83, 123, *136*
Shrew, 61
Sisyrinchium sarmentosum.
    See Blue-eyed-grass
Skunk, **34**, 142
Skunk cabbage (*Lysichiton americanum*), *40*, 67, 68, *126*, *127*
Snake
    blue racer, 18
    garter, 18, 27, 42, 82, 117, 148
    rubber boa, *18*
Snipe, Common, 4, **104**, 131
Snowberry (*Symphoricarpos albus*), *32*, 43, 96, 127, 145, 150

Solanum dulcamara.
    See Nightshade, bittersweet
Solidago spp. See Goldenrod
Solomon's seal, large, false
    (*Maianthemum racemosus*). See False
    Solomon's seal
Sora, 7, *15*, 129
Sorbus sitchensis. See Mountain ash
Sorrel, red. See Dock (*Rumex acetosella*)
Sorrel, wood (*Oxalis oregana*), **67**
Southwood Park, 116
Sparrow
    Chipping, 7
    Dark-eyed Junco, 7, 28, *85*, 99, **136**
    Fox, 56, 101
    Golden-crowned, **28**, 62, 64, 65
    Savannah, 28
    Song, *12*, 28, 48, 56, 62, 64, *80*, **101**
    White-crowned, 56
    White-throated, 65
Spearmint (*Mentha spicata*), *109*, 128
Spiraea douglasii. See Steeple bush
Spirodela polyrhiza. See Duckweed, great
Spring beauty (*Cardamine nuttallii*, small toothwort), 96
Spruce
    blue (*Picea pungens*), 16, 66
    Sitka (*Picea sitchensis*), 17
Spurge, prostrate (*Chamaesyce serpyllifolia*), *70*, 81
Spyglass Park, 60
Squirrel, 11, 98, 106, 110, 116, 149
    Douglas (chickaree), **34,** 53, 62, 113
    flying, 67
    gray, 55, 64
St. John's wort (*Hypericum perforatum*), 6, *122*, **124**
Stachys rigida. See Hedge-nettle
Starflower (*Trientalis latifolia*), 9, 16, **26**, 83
Stark, Brad, 70
Starling, European, 51, 82, *113*, 122
Steeple bush (*Spiraea douglasii*, hard hack), *40*, **41**, *47*, 70, *80*, 85, 113, 129, *138*, 142
Stella Olsen Memorial Park, 126
Stickleback, threespine, 61, 94
Stonegate II Park, 62
Stork's-bill (*Erodium cicutarium*, filaree), 54, **72**
Strawberry, wild (*Fragaria vesca*), 43, 98, 116
Streptopus amplexifolius.
    See Twisted-stalk

Bold = Picture; *Italics* = Description

Bold = Picture; *Italics* = Description

Male Goldfinch on
Himalayan blackberry
Photo by Jim Cruce

Bold = Picture; *Italics* = Description